1-01

VOID

26.00

Spooked

Spooked

Espionage in Corporate America

Adam L. Penenberg
Marc Barry

PERSEUS PUBLISHING
Cambridge, Massachusetts

A CIP record for this book is available from the Library of Congress.

ISBN 0-7382-0271-1

Perseus Publishing is a member of the Perseus Books Group.

Text design by Cynthia Young
Set in 11-point Adobe Berthold Garamond

Perseus Books are available at special discounts for bulk purchases in the U.S. by corporations, institutions, and other organizations. For more information, please contact the Special Markets Department at HarperCollins Publishers, 10 East 53rd Street, New York, NY 10022, or call 1–212–207–7528.

Find us on the World Wide Web at http://www.perseuspublishing.com

1 2 3 4 5 6 7 8 9 10–03 02 01 00
First printing, November 2000

Contents

Author's Note

I first met Marc Barry, my coauthor and founder of the New York–based consulting firm C³I Analytics, while I was researching a story on corporate espionage for the *Forbes* magazine web site. At the time I was pounding out a feature and two sidebars a week, and my usual routine was to spend four days on research and one day drafting stories. Unfortunately that didn't leave much leeway for dead ends. Which is where I found myself when I called Marc.

I had spent the previous three days interviewing a shady character located on the West Coast, and I was having trouble confirming certain facts. The source, a detective, claimed he had used a nifty piece of technology on a caper, which he had secreted away under a photocopier. Three weeks later, dressed as a repairman, he bluffed his way onto the premises again and was able to collect a cache of valuable photocopies from his client's business rival. But no matter how far and wide I searched, I could not find anyone who sold this handy spy gizmo. This made me nervous.

So I phoned Marc, whom I'd been made wise to by a colleague in the newsroom. He fired up his espresso maker, lit up a cigarette, and in a single conversation blew my mind. He told me he had never heard of such a contraption, "but if you find one, Slick, let me know and I'll buy one." I was disappointed. I'd been trying to find a source for a story on corporate espionage for months. Now I had one day of research left before I had to write, and I had diddly squat. Then he said, "You know, corporate espionage is a real growth business."

"Really?" I said.

"Yeah, absolutely. It's the corporate equivalent of a threesome. Lots of people are doing it but no one's admitting it."

"Really . . ." I laughed.

"I mean, ask yourself," he continued, "What happened to all those hardcore spooks after the Berlin Wall came down and the Cold War was over? They had to find jobs somewhere."

Marc started recounting stories about some of his various capers and right there and then I was hooked. Before long, he was putting me in contact with sources I didn't know even existed. It was through him we connected with Karim Fadel, a spy with a guilt complex who works the trade show circuit, and Jan Herring, a former CIA analyst who built the first corporate intelligence unit in history. He put us in touch with Department of Justice attorney Marc Zwillinger, ex-CIA agent McClellan A. ("Guy") Dubois, Teltech researcher Liz Lightfoot, and Charles Hunt, a former assistant director of French Intelligence. He consulted with his own network of National Security Agency (NSA) and Defense Intelligence Agency officials, who provided us with valuable background and insight into the intelligence communities. He explained how he was routinely hired by so-called ethical research companies to get dirt for a client. He demonstrated step by step how he could pull up a target's long-distance phone records and personal credit file. He expounded on techniques he had perfected that enabled him to glean whatever nugget of information he wanted, whenever he wanted it. He regaled me with tales. My favorite: The time he posed as a venture capitalist and flew out to Silicon Valley to meet with the inventor of a hot new technology. When he got to the meeting, he could barely keep from blowing his cover and laughing out loud when he realized everyone in the room, except the inventor, was a corporate spook.

I'd tell you who hired Marc for that one, but I don't know. He is under a nondisclosure agreement (NDA), which ensures his silence under penalty of civil litigation. This also indicated he was a man of his word. After all, if Marc decided to let it slip, who would know? I admired that, although we quickly learned to loathe the term NDA; we knocked heads against it practically every day while researching this book. Thankfully I had a navigator, an insider not only willing to share information, but who ensured its accuracy by putting his name to it. Because of Barry's deep contacts and experience within the spook world, he's also presented as a character in Chapter 4, "The Kite."

Spooked is in no way intended to be a history of business intelligence, nor is it a how-to guide of any sort. Instead it offers a slice of life—through narrative accounts of today's corporate spies—of one of America's fastest growing industries. The stories, though unbelievable, are all very real. The book centers on the first case ever brought to trial under the Economic Espionage Act of 1996, involving glue and label makers Avery Dennison, headquartered in California, and Four Pillars Enterprises of Taiwan. This spy saga began with an Avery scientist who was caught viewing a restricted document and progressed to a joint Avery Dennison–FBI sting operation. This escalated into a flurry of espionage charges and countercharges, with allegations of perjury and prevarication, entrapment, evidence- and jury-tampering, kidnapping, and misuse of the federal penal code thrown in for good measure. It is a case that raises the disturbing question: Could a powerful American company misuse federal law to decapitate a foreign rival as a part of its global business strategy?

The Avery Dennison incident is not the result of an isolated episode. You'll read about the PictureTel spook, who uses his tricks to soak up some of his competitors' most precious secrets. Former CIA agent Jan Herring tells the history of information collection at Motorola. Hacker Marc Maiffret explains how he was once paid $1,000 to steal U.S. military software by a Kashmiri terrorist linked with Osama bin Laden. Liz Lightfoot shows the kind of data she can dig up with just a phone, a computer, and a modem.

A couple of months into researching this book, I called Marc to run a potential source by him, a corporate spy type who had cold-called me at *Forbes* magazine with a tale of intrigue. But something didn't feel right. I just couldn't put my finger on it.

"He claims he's former CIA," I said.

Marc roared when he heard the name. "Slick, he's CIA, all right. He probably worked in the *cafeteria*. Seriously. A lot of these clowns? They say they work for a three-lettered agency like CIA, FBI, or NSA? Well, there's no easy way to tell, since no intelligence agency will ever tell you if some guy ever worked for them."

"The cafeteria," I repeated.

"Aren't you glad I'm working with you?"

Sure. Without Marc Barry there would be no *Spooked*.

Prologue

Spy Trap

Pin Yen (P. Y.) Yang, a seventy-two-year-old Taiwanese businessman and founder of Four Pillars Enterprises, leafed through papers marked "CONFIDENTIAL" and "Property of Avery Dennison" and pried out the staples. It was a hot, suffocating day in early September 1997, and Yang, his daughter Sally (a researcher at Four Pillars), and Avery Dennison scientist Ten Hong (Victor) Lee were in the Westlake Holiday Inn in Cleveland, Ohio. There they sipped Dr. Pepper and munched on blueberry bagels (for Yang an exotic food), discussed obstacles in producing pressure-sensitive adhesives, peppering their four-hour conversation with words like "tackifier," "viscosity," and "high-speed release"—and engaged in what the government would later call economic espionage.

Each time Yang came across the confidential warnings stamped on a patent application for a new Avery technology—an environmentally friendly adhesives process that was also cost-efficient—and on a secret plan outlining expansion into Asia, he folded over the pages, made a crease, then slit it with a pocket knife. Yang was particularly disturbed by the patent application, which covered the rights to an all-purpose, or universal, "acrylic emulsion adhesive." It looked similar to a technology his company had developed. Yang had been involved in some contentious battles over patents in the past and he figured this might presage the latest chapter. Since no stapler was handy, after each cut Yang taped the pages back together like a hinge. Indicating the more than dozen damning paper scraps, he addressed Lee, his "consultant": "You have to throw that trash out at your home," Yang told him in Taiwanese. "Take that back to your house." The last thing he needed was to be detained by U.S. Customs with pages stamped "CONFIDENTIAL" and "Property of Avery Dennison." That could mean big trouble.

"All right," Lee replied. Treating Yang like a dear uncle, he indicated Yang's bagel and said, "Eat it fresh, the next day it won't be good." The conversation continued in this friendly vein, covering Lee's daughter's PSAT scores, colleges, the word for "fungus" in Taiwanese ("Mei Jun"), and the fact that most Taiwanese graduate students resist learning English, the language of science. Ten minutes later Yang handed some papers to his daughter. "Why don't you take care of these," he said in a mixture of Mandarin and Taiwanese. "I think I only need this part." Sally cut out the confidential markings.

For the Yangs, meeting with Lee had become something of a ritual. Although Yang did visit America, it was usually Lee, a naturalized American born in Taiwan, who would trek to his homeland during the summer with his family on all-expense-paid trips where he was treated as visiting royalty. He dropped off adhesives literature, books, and research papers. He gave lectures on the science of glue, providing, the government would allege, detailed disclosures of Avery's confidential materials, including copies of new products and process ideas in the experimental phase. He handed off specifications Lee himself claimed were "extremely confidential." Then he picked up his bounty, which Four Pillars hid by depositing it into Lee's sister-in-law's bank account in Taiwan or by paying him in traveler's checks.

But this time was different. At the behest of agents of the Federal Bureau of Investigation, Lee had requested that Yang and his daughter visit him in America. Yang, on his way to see tennis star Michael Chang play at the U.S. Open in Flushing, New York, planned his itinerary to include Cleveland. The hotel room had been wired with microphones and a hidden camera. A phalanx of FBI agents, led by special agent in charge Michael Bartholomew, were watching the whole thing unfold over closed-circuit TV. Ten months earlier Lee, in an earlier sting operation, had been videotaped by the FBI trying to steal a bogus Asian expansion plan—the same plan Yang now possessed. When confronted, Lee confessed and became the government's star snitch, although not an overly cooperative one.

For seven years Lee had been paid $25,000 annually by Four Pillars to slip the company information about adhesives, including, the government would allege, a battery-label laminate Avery created for Duracell's PowerCheck battery, a chemical formula for diaper tape, complex recipes for adhesives, and samples of Avery products in development. In 1989 alone, his first year working for Four Pillars, Lee sent fourteen mailings and had become so attached to his sideline business with Four Pillars that he would use "we" in his correspondence with Yang & Co., as if his job at Avery were a mere afterthought.

To many whose idea of glue may be Elmer's, adhesive formulae may sound pretty mundane. In fact it is a cutthroat industry driven by research and development: It is a company's comparative advantage, raising high barriers to entry. Warp speed technological change makes it difficult for the little guy to keep up, even one like Four Pillars, which was the number one adhesives seller in Taiwan and a strong force in mainland China, with $160 million in annual sales. One self-adhesive material can have up to twelve layers of separate chemicals, each with a different function, feature, or capability. Each layer must be within a precise tolerance for thickness and coverage; it can't be too wet, or too dry, otherwise it will fall off or won't last; manufacturing and production has to be finely tuned and managed carefully. For Avery Dennison, 75 percent of its business relates to pressure-sensitive adhesives, the stuff that makes peel-off labels peel off without leaving your fingers sticky. Its founder, R. Stanton Avery, formulated the first commercially viable self-adhesive label in 1935 and founded an entire industry. Now a $3.2 billion business, Avery supplies the labels used by the Internal Revenue Service on form 1040 and peel-and-stick postage stamps, and its products are an unheralded yet profitable part of jeans, photographic film containers, price tags, and shampoo bottles. The company is also a big player in the automotive, electronic, and medical markets. To stay ahead, the company plows money into its research and development (R&D). From 1993 to 1996 alone, the company invested more than $200 million into research.

Lee, a naturalized American citizen who got his Ph.D. in chemical engineering from Texas Tech and a master's of science degree in polymer science from the University of Akron, pilfered ten formulas from Avery, passing them to Four Pillars. An expert in methods to make pressure-sensitive adhesives stick to various surfaces under different conditions, Lee even used Avery Dennison labs to compare and test Four Pillars' products against Avery's, then offered advice on how his adopted company could improve its wares to compete more effectively. This earned him additional income and the one thing he seemed to crave more than anything: respect. It also catapulted him into a heap of trouble, from which he tried to extricate himself by becoming a "flipper," someone who cooperates with the law to avoid prosecution or lessen any potential penalties.

Just before packing up to leave, Yang unwittingly mentioned an FBI sting he'd heard about. Three months earlier, a Bureau operation run out of the Four Seasons Hotel in Philadelphia resulted in the arrest of two Taiwanese nationals working for the Yuen Foong

Paper Co. Ltd., both of whom had ties to the Taiwanese govern-ment. They were charged with attempting to buy Bristol-Myers's process for bioengineering the anticancer drug Taxol for $400,000, a bargain if they had gotten away with it, since the information was worth billions. Not surprisingly, the case attracted a lot of media coverage in Taiwan.

America, Sally pointed out, now "has a special division to catch business spies."

"I am a very careful person," Yang said. "Whatever I get I get rid of immediately. I don't like to make phone calls, so [Sally] called you, but I wouldn't. When you come to Taipei it would be all right to meet you to talk. You can collect or get some new samples, or the new research trends. Whatever tomorrow's product, we have to develop it earlier. . . . We do not need to copy the thing. We can modify it."

Yang looked around the room one last time: "We didn't forget anything?" he asked. They slipped out, and Lee drove them to Cleveland Hopkins International Airport. He had played his part perfectly. He had been the model stool pigeon. Neither Yang nor Sally noticed the car trailing them to the airport, nor, when they arrived at the departures terminal, the two cars holding federal agents already parked by Continental Airlines.

Lee said his good-byes, let them out of the car, dropped their luggage at the curb—to the end, the dutiful servant—and agents swooped in for the arrest.

I

The Intelligencing of Corporate America

When the FBI learned Edward O'Malley had been invited to a conference in France to give a talk on the newly passed Economic Espionage Act of 1996, Bureau brass asked him to carry a message. Tell the French government and spy community the rules have changed, they said. Tell them the Bureau takes the act seriously and plans to enforce it. Tell them the United States would not look the other way anymore if a foreign company or government tried to steal U.S. corporate secrets.

O'Malley was an apt choice to act as emissary. Not only was he a former FBI chief of counterintelligence, he was famous for helping IBM nail a Japanese competitor in a complex sting operation in the early 1980s. This resulted in two employees of Hitachi pleading guilty to conspiring to transport stolen documents and components for IBM's then-snazziest generation of computers. "Meetings between Hitachi officials and our undercover IBM agent showed Hitachi officials saying, 'Yes, we want to beat IBM to market,' and caught the Hitachi officials paying $650,000 for the information,"

O'Malley says. "It was then easy for the feds to come in and arrest them."

After skimming the tarmac at Charles de Gaulle International Airport the former G-man gave his briefing, noting "a certain amount of discomfort," he says. "I told the audience the act was not aimed at CI [competitive intelligence] professionals. It was aimed at those who steal corporate trade secrets. Collecting can be done legitimately, but stealing is not okay."

There was some Franco-style grumbling, and someone who identified himself as being from DGSE, France's version of the CIA, asked a few questions. O'Malley characterizes the tone as "hostile." Afterward O'Malley was invited to give a personal briefing to a retired French general, accompanied by a colonel. He briefed them on the new law, the same presentation he had given earlier.

When he finished, the general asked for a copy of the act. "Now let me give you a message to take back with you," he told O'Malley with the imperiousness of a nobleman addressing an errand boy. "If you Americans enforce this act, we French will retaliate against American corporations who are stealing French corporate secrets."

As an intelligence professional O'Malley knew that France, the nation that put the "gall" in Gallic, had no intention of curtailing its corporate espionage activities. Three former heads of DGSE openly admitted that France engaged in spying on American business and that computer hacking is illegal only if the victim is located on French soil. But France hasn't been the only ally sifting through American corporate R&D, it has just been the most open about it.

A 1997 report to Congress compiled by the CIA, FBI, and military intelligence grabbers concluded that foreign government–backed corporate espionage "poses a direct threat to the health and competitiveness of the U.S. economy." Repeat offenders: China, France, Japan, the United Kingdom, Mexico and Russia, South Korea and Taiwan. Although it is not on the list, you can add Israel, too. "We have an agreement with Israel not to spy, though they spy on us, so it's b.s.," says Guy Dubois, former chief of the CIA's operations group Committee on Imagery Requirements and Exploitation, which specializes in industrial counter-espionage. "With the possible exception of the British, American intelligence has no friends."

Now more than ever corporations rely on information about competitors—their products, strategies, marketing, pricing, and corporate leadership. It is often the difference between a fat, happy hundred-million-dollar company and bankruptcy. Of course, if you are the victim, it can be the difference between suffering bankruptcy and being that fat, happy hundred-million-dollar company.

The U.S. Chamber of Commerce believes espionage has led to losses to corporate shareholders of about $25 billion a year in intellectual property. But companies are reluctant to report info-breaches, afraid of public humiliation or that shareholders will hold them accountable and mount multimillion-dollar class-action suits. They are also leery of being forced to divulge even more information about their tightly held secrets in the discovery phase of a trial. So the usual victim strategy is to do nothing except try to correct the security flaws. Normally corporate espionage is written off as a cost of doing business. This has made it easy for America's allies and enemies alike.

Israeli and Chinese spies are notorious for setting up front companies to purchase technology they are barred from obtaining on the up and up. Israel, for example, was not able to purchase high-speed computers on the open market because of the belief they could be diverted to the plucky desert nation's nuclear arsenal, so it found alternative methods. One blown operation: In 1987 a group of Israelis went to negotiate a joint venture with Lockheed Saunders, an electronics firm in New Jersey. One of the Israelis was in the process of leaving the plant when he had a problem with his briefcase. The lock flipped open to reveal a hidden camera and stash of film. Lockheed didn't bother to press charges. Instead, following the usual corporate protocol, guards confiscated the camera and film and kicked the group out.

Similar spy strategies aren't all Israel and China have in common. A lot of Israeli military technology has ended up in China. Israel's high-tech industry assisted the Chinese in developing infrared and electri-optical sights for its tanks and helped them retrofit MIG-21s (the Chinese call them F-7s) with an upgraded electronics package. Israel's tech sector has traditionally maintained close ties with the Israeli Defense Force, which is always looking for ways to raise cash. That is why it sometimes acts as middleman for Israeli industry, as it did with China's military, and the reason you find Israeli commandos training military groups in Africa. It is also how American R&D ends up in Israeli high-tech companies, who are eager to continue their miracle in the desert in cyberspace. It is a main reason there are more Israeli companies listed on the NASDAQ exchange than all of Europe combined: this cycle of information.

As far as spying on allies goes, however, Israel doesn't hold a candle to France, which has no peers. Competivite intelligence professionals—called CI in spook speak—advise clients to avoid French airlines because it's generally accepted that conversations are recorded and flight attendants are trained in information elicitation techniques. French not-so-secret agents are famous for conducting what are called "black bag jobs," breaking into the Paris hotel rooms of foreign executives and copying documents.

But the French aren't just renowned for spying on visitors to their country. A different kind of black bag job took place on American soil in 1991, when two men were spotted heaving trash bags into the back of a van in front of the home of a Texas Instruments executive. The van's license number was subsequently traced to the French consulate in Houston. What was the French government's response? The consul general calmly explained he and an aide had been out collecting grass clippings–grass clippings. And in January 2000, French Intelligence was caught eavesdropping on executives from British Aerospace, British Petroleum, and British Airways who dared to talk business over their cell phones while in their own country.

France has also made use of stolen American corporate R&D: After Motorola inked a deal in 1979 for the manufacture of a sixteen-bit advanced microprocessor by, among others, Societe pour l'Etude & la Fabrication de Circuits Integres Speciaux, a company owned jointly by Thomson CSF, a French military and electronics behemoth, and Commissariat a l'Energie Atomique, the French Atomic Energy Commission, Thomson would transform itself into a major player in semiconductors. A number of media outlets have reported that DGSE recruited former European employees of IBM, Texas Instruments, and other electronics firms for debriefing, then submitted their information to Compagnie des Machines Bull, a computer firm largely owned by the French government.

Although the French have been the most aggressive, Japan has turned business intelligence into a fine art: "The Japanese are the professionals," says former CIA agent Jan Herring, founder of the Society of Competitive Intelligence Professionals (SCIP), a trade organization. "They're the ones who started it. They do it almost second nature. It's just part of their companies." Mitsui, the giant Japanese trading company, has as its corporate motto, "Information is the lifeblood of the company," and it means it. Even back in the days before e-mail transformed corporate communication, the firm's internal network conveyed some 80,000 messages a day, many of them containing competitor intelligence between 200 offices worldwide via satellite. Companies like Mitsui and Mitsubishi also reap assistance from the Japanese government. Both the Ministry of International Trade and Industry (MITI) and Japan External Trade Organization glean prodigious amounts of commercial information, translate and analyze it, then share it with whole industries. MITI even started a school for corporate spying in 1962, called the Institute for Industrial Protection.

One way the Japanese have funneled technology from the United States is by placing key people in organizations like the National Institutes of Health and National Bureau of Standards and assigning them the important job of deciding the standards that allow machines to talk to one another. "If you look at Japanese R&D, it is focused on applied research," Dubois says. "But a large share of American research is blue-sky, which requires a lot of cooperation between corporations, education, and government. The Japanese tried to get broadened access to it and used it as the basis to develop commercial products."

The U.S. Commerce Department found that foreign-owned companies often cluster in high-tech corridors near universities and corporate research facilities, where new ideas and technologies percolate. The 1995 Commerce Department report estimated that foreign corporations spent more than $14.6 billion on R&D at 645 foreign-owned facilities in the United States, including 75 in New Jersey, of all places. Why Jersey? It is a center for the nation's pharmaceutical industry, where a quarter of all foreign spending on R&D in the United States takes place. Silicon Valley and North Carolina's Research Triangle also had high concentrations of foreign companies, who said their top two reasons for choosing these particular locations was to "acquire technology" and "keep abreast of technological development." The response "Engage in basic research" ended up near the bottom of the list.

If this has been the behavior of America's allies, how have its enemies treated its businesses? Like one giant R&D laboratory.

In the early 1980s a reliable CIA operative high up in the KGB food chain passed Dubois stunning information: a list of 100 top technology companies that Soviet Intelligence had been targeting in a massive technology transfer program involving the whole Warsaw Pact. To Dubois it read like a KGB wish list: General Electric, Boeing, Lockheed, Hewlett-Packard, GTE, Sperry, Honeywell, IBM, Westinghouse, Digital Equipment Corp.

The Soviet's objective was to funnel technology from the West so it could achieve military-technical parity. The industries the KGB targeted were at the heart of America's military-industrial complex: electronics; armor and electro-optics; aviation; missiles and space; projectiles and explosives; communications and chemicals; radars and computers. The CIA believed this corporate spy strategy was instrumental in the Soviets squeezing America's lead in certain key tech industries like microelectronics from twelve years to six. It also helped them create carbon copies of hot American military technology. The Soviet AWACS and space shuttles were almost exact duplicates of America's original models. The Soviet AN-72, an exact copy of the prototype for Boeing's short take-off and landing technology, was deployed in the Russian arsenal just sixteen months after it had been invented. And where did the original missile guidance system technology used in the Russian fighter that shot down Korean Air Line's Flight 007 in 1983 come from? The United States.

The material was so extensive and so inside, did Dubois ever fear he was being fed disinformation by his KGB plant? "No, not with this source," he says. "I had 100 percent confidence the information was good." Dubois went to work on a CIA white paper. In it, he characterized the Soviet technological transfer program as "massive and global," which had successfully closed the technology gap with the West. William Casey, then head of the CIA, liked it so much he asked Dubois to circulate the paper within the agency for comment. All the internal CIA reviews were positive, except one. Duane "Dewey" Clarridge, CIA chief of European operations, called Dubois to tell him the report was "a crashing bore." Clarridge suggested spiking it with some forged documents that implicated the Soviets in going after four or five companies in the UK, to influence the British government.

Clarridge, who single-handedly mined harbors in Nicaragua in the covert war against the Sandinistas and would eventually be forced to testify during Iran/contra, wanted more sex and violence in the report. Dubois refused. Their disagreement escalated to the point that both were ordered into Bill Casey's office, with Casey, in a forty-five-minute meeting, eventually siding with Dubois. Even without Clarridge's sexing it up, *Soviet Acquisition of Western Technology*, published in 1982, became a global best-seller and was translated into five languages.

According to Dubois, one major diversion program initiated by the Soviets involved microelectronic technology. Tapping unscrupulous Western traders eager to bid for the KGB's usual 500 percent markups, the Soviets were able to set up some 400 dummy corporations in Europe alone, with a number of others in the United States. They provided falsified licenses and deceptive equipment descriptions and lied about who would ultimately receive the technology. This way the Soviets were able to acquire enough equipment and technology to architect almost its entire microelectronic industry, from material preparation to design and fabrication to final testing of chips to the creation of whole lines of computers.

In 1982 U.S. Customs officials came across a cache of laser components and sophisticated electronics in a divorcee's garage in Redwood City, California, a suburb of San Francisco. They charged Millie McKee with attempting to illegally export her glitzy high-tech stash to Switzerland, where authorities believed it would be rerouted to the Soviet Union. Her penalty: six months in work release for providing a false statement, which she characterized as "technical violations," like driving over the speed limit. Three years later Italian national Marino Pradetto, who operated with a West German electronics firm, was arrested at a trade show in California and charged with illegal diversion of the VAX II/780 mainframe computer to Czechoslovakia via a circuitous shipping route: San Jose, Haiti, and Switzerland.

As the final days of the Cold War dragged to an end, the FBI estimated a third of Russian diplomats were involved in espionage. One early 1980s Soviet spy hub was situated in a brick building with a whitewashed roof and a sweeping view of San Francisco Bay. Not only was the setting beautiful, it was perfect for receiving unobstructed microwave signals. The building housed some forty Soviet officials, a lot for a city this size, but they were not sitting on the dock of San Francisco Bay to boost Soviet tourism. The antennae on the roof were hooked into electronic wizardry that could grab whole conversations out of the air when it recognized certain words or phrases. But the Soviet's tried and true method was to turn a corporate insider into a mole, and it didn't limit its spying on the United States. Between 1967 and 1984 the KGB received data on the "Tornado" aircraft manufactured by the European Panavia consortium from West German citizen Manfred Rotsch, head of the planning department of the aviation firm Messerschmitt-Bolkow-Blohm. Deiter Gerhardt, a South African naval officer who had served at the embassy in London, passed another Soviet spy division, the GRU, information on a number of antiaircraft missiles.

Not all of these operations were the product of KGB guile. Eastern European spy services in Poland and the former Czechoslovakia and East Germany were often more successful than their Soviet counterparts. Poland's intelligence service turned two spy stunners. The CIA believes Poland saved the Soviets several tens of millions of rubles in research efforts and advanced the state of radar technology between 1978 and 1981 when it made a traitor out of William Bell, an American radar specialist working for Hughes Aircraft Company. Bell's expertise was in advanced and experimental U.S. radar systems and air-to-air and surface-to-air missiles. Poland also flipped James Harper, an electronics engineer whose wife had access to Ballistic Missile Defense Advanced Technology Center contracts at Systems Control Inc., California. Over a ten-year period starting in 1971, Harper turned over dozens of documents relating to potential U.S. ballistic missile programs and ICBM basing modes.

The program was so successful the Soviet Union abandoned the idea of producing its own computers. For its Kremlin mainframe RIAD computer the Russians cloned IBM's 360 and 370 mainframe series, and the Apple II had its nameplate switched to the Soviet AGAT personal computer. From the late 1970s to the end of the Cold War, the Soviets siphoned off perhaps as many as 30,000 pieces of high-tech equipment and 400,000 technical documents, which, according to then-assistant secretary of defense Richard Perle, helped it to slice America's lead in technology from ten years to as little as three. What the Soviet Union couldn't steal, it bought. In 1979 and 1981, it received two dry docks from Sweden and Japan, agreeing to use them only for commercial shipping. Shortly after they were converted to military use in aircraft carriers.

Stealing industrial secrets is not new, of course. In 1811 Francis Cabot Lowell traveled to England and ripped off the plans for the Cartwright loom, which he memorized while touring a factory. With it, Lowell, who was rewarded for his coup with the naming of a Massachusetts town after him, brought home the blueprints for America's industrial revolution. The Soviets got started later, in the 1930s, when Communist agents swiped Eastman Kodak's process for developing color pictures. By the 1960s, as the United

States began to alter the strategic military balance with more accurate missiles, Soviet information collecting was redirected to high tech. Former U.S. Navy admiral Bobby Ray Inman, the former deputy director of the CIA, believed the Kremlin waited until the bugs were worked out of a particular weapon before going after it. Toward the end, though, they became more interested in uncovering the theory behind a particular technology instead of merely copying it.

After Dubois published his white paper he went on a road show, offering presentations to some of the targeted companies. "I remember being at Boeing in Seattle, where I put up a slide with six technologies the Soviets wanted," Dubois says. "The Soviets had captured specifications on semiconductors, how to slice silicon wafers, and knew exactly how the components worked. A guy in the audience stands up and says, 'It's not possible. Those technologies come from my department.' He just couldn't believe it. I told Boeing the Soviets clearly had some gaps to fill, which is why I was addressing them."

These presentations, however, shouldn't be confused with the CIA passing information to an American company. That is against the agency's stated mission, Dubois says. "We have given American companies briefings on industrial developments and exchanged information, like when a company has been targeted by a foreign entity. But has the CIA ever walked into Boeing and said, 'Airbus just got a $40 million subsidy from the government under the table?' No."

That may have been true in Dubois's day—he left the CIA in 1998 after serving twenty-six years. Nowadays, as more government agents move to the private sector while maintaining close contact with their former colleagues, the line between America's government and its corporations is beginning to blur, especially at the NSA, which has been maintaining secret corporate connections.

On January 1, 1999, strategists from Eastman Kodak, Coca-Cola, GTE, Mitre Corporation, Mobile Oil, and Boeing, along with agents from the CIA, FBI, DIA, NSA, and DoD were all present during an NSA briefing. Entitled "The Generic Intelligence Training Initiative," the presentation featured the National Security Agency's Nomogenisis Project, an Internet-based training module. Nomogenisis strived to teach intelligence analysts how to collect and assemble random intelligence data from many different sources, share it amongst themselves, and assemble it into a mosaic-like picture. It also improved the analysts' ability to correctly interpret the subtext of the intelligence they analyzed in order to understand a target's true intentions. Reading the subtext correctly allows an analyst to predict the target's next move in order to develop more accurate intelligence forecasts.

As a result, America shouldn't expect much sympathy from its allies. Former DGSE deputy chief Charles Hunt is quick to chastise the United States for condemning other nations for espionage and has no problem with governments assisting industry in the global marketplace. He says he is just being realistic when he claims no company is ethical. Hunt claims both IBM and Hewlett stole technology from French company Thomson CSF for microchips hardy enough to withstand a nuclear blast. "But of course when companies like IBM, HP, Motorola, and Thomson sign cross-agreements, it's often hard to know who's guilty," he admits. Hunt points out that in 1995 France requested that five Americans, including the CIA's station chief and four diplomats, exit the country. He says all five Americans worked for the CIA and had expressed keen interest in France's positions on the General Agreement on Tariffs and Trade (GATT) and telecommunications. What he neglected to mention was that during his tenure at DGSE between 1981 and 1983, Hunt, under the direction of DGSE director Pierre Marion, built a unit within his spy organization dedicated to industrial espionage.

What does Hunt do now that he isn't leading France's secret agents? In a story as implausible as his accent is thick, he claims he is merely "a businessman not involved with international politics" nor "with anything that involves EEA [Economic Espionage Act]," despite being labeled a Silicon Valley spy by a local newspaper. In other words, he has taken his skills to the private sector, working as a consultant.

Suave guys like Hunt go against the stereotype of the corporate spook. When people think of corporate espionage they generally envision a trench coat–clad character picking the lock at a lab, slipping past the night watchman, and stealing the secret formula for a new billion-dollar elixir. But that's Hollywood. There are far more subtle ways for a spy like him to achieve his objective, without exposing himself to that level of risk, methods that have served him and those like him for generations. Today CI is just as clever and ruthless as anything any government has ever pulled. That's because former intelligence agents like Hunt play the same game but for different stakes. Like him, corporate intelligence professionals are far less imposing than in the bitter days of the Cold War; they are often likeable guys, with a contagious laugh and disarming wit, great storytellers with anecdotes to spare. But beneath the surface they can be ruthless, methodical predators who live by deception and manipulation. Often they are trained by government agencies and would never resort to something as clumsy as breaking and entering to pluck a diamond from the rough. A spy trained by the CIA in advanced human elicitation techniques can glean the information he craves from a target company's employees, contractors, and vendors. He might be the happy-go-lucky caller to the accounts payable department who just needs a "minor clarification" on the identity of a certain new supplier. He may appear on the green at a country club where he is invited to play nine holes with the orthopedic surgeon who just happens to be in charge of conducting clinical trials on the target's new pain medication about to be sent to the FDA for approval. He could be a graduate student calling for information on a particular industrial process for his dissertation.

Like Hunt, Americans working for the CIA, NSA, FBI, Defense Intelligence Agency, and military intelligence have found lucrative positions awaiting them after their public service is complete. Dubois spent a quarter of a centurey in the CIA before taking a job with Raytheon. Now he is with Imagery Geospatial Systems, located in the D.C. tech corridor. Dubois's old boss, Jan Herring, runs his own consultancy; another pillar of the CI industy, John Nolan, is what he calls "a former federal intelligence officer" and owns Phoenix Consulting group; and William Degenaro ran 3M's spook division before founding his own CI firm in Sarasota, Florida. In the twenty or so years since these first agents arrived on the scene, there has been a gradual acceptance of intelligence operations as a necessary part of everyday corporate life. This has led to the creation of a real growth industry, with ex-cops, detectives, database librarians, lawyers, and even accountants putting out a spook shingle.

It is the intelligencing of corporate America.

But it was the fall of the Berlin Wall in 1989 that launched CI into the stratosphere. The collapse of America's Cold War foe threw a lot of spies out of work, victims of downsizing. Without a worthy adversary, the U.S. intelligence community was streamlined. Unemployed spooks pounded the pavement in search of work. At the same time, American industry was getting slaughtered in the global marketplace. It wasn't long before the two groups found each other. Although American corporations were apprehensive at first, it was an easy transition to the private sector for the spies. And though the ground rules had changed and the capers were now commercial instead of ideological, the same techniques applied and a new industry arose from the Wall's rubble.

Between 1985 and 1989 the CIA Science and Technology unit worked directly with American companies to train and educate executives on modern intelligence collection methods. The CIA claims this training was purely of a counterintelligence nature, designed to be defensive, not offensive. Shortly after receiving this CIA-sponsored training, however, corporate CI departments began to blossom, and in several instances CIA agents were hired away from the agency to run them.

Shortly after their arrival at their new dream jobs—the jobs that paid boatloads of money—the jobs that allowed the freedom to traverse places the government would never allow, the spooks soon realized their new employers had a more domestic agenda. American executives were more interested in their American competitors than their rivals abroad. A CEO might say, "Yeah, we certainly should keep an eye on those Japanese and French, but frankly we're more interested in what DuPont across the street is working on." Instead of taking on foreign spies, million-dollar budgets were established and American companies began waging war, using internal CI departments hidden from public and shareholder scrutiny, many with seemingly innocuous titles—External Development, Market Research, and Strategic Marketing.

Since the 1980s, the intelligencing of corporate America has gone mainstream. And this is why Hunt is so critical. "How can American corporations complain about spying when they too are spying?" he asks.

Case in point: Small apparel company Johnston Industries Inc. versus large apparel maker Milliken & Co. According to a lawsuit filed by Johnston in 1998, Milliken, one of the largest textile makers in the country with, $2 billion in annual sales, hired two Atlanta detective firms, Global Intelligence Inc. and R. A. Taylor & Associates, to lift customer lists, financial records, and product development research, which they did over a two-year period beginning in 1995. The suit alleged that the owner of both detective agencies, Rodney Taylor, boldly posed as an investment banker representing Swiss investors interested in getting into the apparel game and held a meeting with then-president of Johnston, Gerald Andrews. Relying on southern charm and guile, Taylor was given unfettered access to some of Johnston's top executives and secret documents and given personal tours of the factories.

At the same time, one of Taylor's employees, Justin Waldrep, contacted Johnston Industries, claiming to be a graduate student at Georgia State University who needed to learn more about the apparel business for his master's thesis. He promised that no one outside of his professor would ever read what he wrote. In the southern textile business, assisting students conducting research is common.

As it turned out, Waldrep was never a student at Georgia State, but he was so convincing Johnston executives didn't bother checking up on him. As a result, Waldrep was taken around to plants in Alabama and Georgia and encouraged to interview several company officials and even customers. Johnston, a company with $330 million in annual sales, makes tablecloths and napkins, as well as material used to cover seats in cars and planes, plus bedding, furniture, and other products. In the end, it claims, this elegant little scam cost the company $30 million, with the impostors stealing the formula for a superabsorbent polyester fabric that had pushed up Johnston's linen sales.

How did this napkin and tablecloth maker catch the crooks? It didn't. According to current Johnston Industries president D. Ogle Clark, "We came across a lawsuit filed [by NRB, another textile maker] against Milliken and was surprised to see our name in there. Then we realized we'd suffered the same thing." The scam had been so good the mid-size textile maker hadn't even known it had been taken. The biggest difference in the two like incidents was that Waldrep had given his college affiliation as Columbia University Business School to NRB.

Less surreptitious schemes are fairly common. In June 2000, Oracle acknowledged it had hired Investigative Group International (IGI), a detective agency founded by former Watergate prosecutor Terry Lenzner, to investigate groups sympathetic to Microsoft, an effort that produced material embarrassing to Microsoft at a most inopportune time: while the software heavyweight battled antitrust allegations in court. The investigation came to light when IGI operatives tried to bribe janitors at the pro-Microsoft trade group, the Association for Competitive Technology. What did they want? The group's trash. A month earlier, Time Warner admitted it had engaged in corporate espionage when managers in Houston, Texas, sponsored an in-house intelligence gathering operation. Employees received a flier with their paychecks, giving them either free Internet service or the chance to win $100. The flier offered a caveat: "To qualify we need your help in accomplishing our objective which is to locate areas of Houston that Southwestern Bell (our competitor) can and cannot service their high-speed online service." To qualify for the reward, Time Warner workers had to order high-speed Internet access from Southwestern Bell, cancel if it was confirmed, then report back to the Houston office. Time Warner PR czars admitted it had been a mistake; Southwestern Bell called it fraudulent and anticompetitive.

Notwithstanding the bad PR from cases like this that bubble over into the public because of a lawsuit, the American CI industry's governing body, the Society of Competitive Intelligence Professionals (SCIP) boasts 7,000 members and is reaping the rewards of a successful ten-year campaign designed to put a warm, fuzzy veneer on collection activities. SCIP's rhetoric is designed to put corporate clients more at ease with the idea of spying on their competitors by stressing the "ethical" acquisition of information—

from publicly available or "open source" materials like published material, public filings, patents, and annual reports.

The purpose of SCIP's spin control is to make industrial spying less shocking and therefore more palatable to a larger cross section of corporate America. Members of the organization agree to abide by SCIP ethical rules, which prohibit misrepresentation or deception when interviewing a member of a competitor on behalf of a client. Of course that doesn't mean that there aren't cliques. SCIP meetings have been known to resemble a junior high school dance. On one side you have hardcore former spooks trained by the CIA, FBI, and DIA and on the other side you have the database librarians.

Today, even Ernst & Young, a mammoth accounting firm with an extremely conservative history, openly boasts of a sixty-member intelligence unit whose services are readily available to any E&Y client wishing to know what its competitors are up to. Deloit & Touche have hired former CIA agents to run its CI department. Indeed, intelligence has become so broadly accepted that Mercy Hearst College in Pennsylvania offers a four-year program that serves as a training ground for aspiring corporate intelligence agents.

Despite their self-imposed voluntary ethical guidelines, however, some SCIP members have acted positively CIA-like, collecting intelligence on their own clients and illegally purchasing and selling targets' credit reports and telephone records. One brilliant scam: A SCIP member from Israel teaches a corporate intelligence class to executives from top American companies. To get in, however, the would-be student has to fill out an elaborate application that elicits information about his company. The belief is that the teacher, who has dual citizenship in Israel and is a former member of the Israel Secret Police, is collecting information on his students, then passing it to the Israeli Mossad.

These types of ethical violations have not been committed by underlings but by pillars of the SCIP community, as well as by SCIP board members. In the event that a particular operation has the potential to turn ugly, and distance between the company and the operation is required, the job is subcontracted to special consultants, or "kites," as they are known. The kite serves as a proxy. He does the dirty work but provides plausible deniablity to a company in case an operation goes awry. Essentially he is flown out on his own to gather sensitive intelligence information by any means necessary, doing the things a company cannot do itself because the risk is too great.

A kite, through a process called "running tolls," may illegally acquire copies of a CEO's cell or residential telephone bill, or even clone his pager. He does not think twice about handing over illegal credit reports of a competitor's key management personnel. In addition to the data a kite provides, of equal importance is plausible deniability. If the operation is discovered, a criminal investigation initiated, or a lawsuit levied, the company can claim ignorance by claiming the offender was an independent contractor, not an employee. That way it can claim the contractor was operating independently.

Kites are not merely hired for their expertise; they also come fully equipped with the latest gadgets. One such tool is known as an "answering machine pick," a device that grabs messages off a target's telephone answering machine. The spy can dial any phone number with an answering machine on the other end and, when it answers, the pick sequentially replicates the tones of the telephone keypad until it breaks the security code, enabling the user to download messages. Another interesting toy: Raytheon's "Silent Runner." Originally developed for the NSA, Silent Runner is an Internet monitoring device that acts like a computer hacker surveillance program when placed on a corporate network. It can rummage around and let the user monitor all incoming and outgoing e-mail traffic and view activity on individual computer screens, as well as document the architecture of a competitor's corporate infrastructure.

These are just a few samples. In recent years an entire spy tech industry has sprouted. Military contractor Raytheon is working with Barry's CI firm, C³I Analytics, to retrofit military technology from the U.S. Army's Land Information Warfare Activity facility for use in CI. They are building a corporate "war room" in New York City equipped with banks of high-speed computers and state-of-the-art satellite surveillance hardware for a cool $7 million. They plan to sell services to corporations intent on studying the enemy's every move. Through videoconferencing the war room will be able to support 500 people in 500 different locations around the globe who can converse and share data in real time, displayed on a six-by twenty-foot video screen. It also comes with a spinning three-dimensional hologram of the world displaying rotating satellites, and thirty work stations for crunching complex data.

A number of Internet sites, with names like Spy Tech Agency and SurveillanceSupplies.com, offer whole catalogs of spy tools available at a click. For $59.95 the Elite Outbound Call Register can log the numbers and dates of all outgoing calls. The Tele-Monitor 2001 lets the user listen in via regular telephone lines from anywhere; it runs $219.85. A wireless microphone system with a range of 250 feet goes for $319.95 (which includes Velcro for covert mounting). The Under-Door Scope with night-vision attachment lets someone on the outside observe an entire room inside from the floor up for $4,849.95. And for those who really want to keep tabs on the competition, a GPS Digital Tracking System allows a target to be secretly tracked anywhere in the world. Price: $5,995.95.

But why should companies restrict themselves to knowing what the competition is up to today when they can hire Advanced Competitive Strategies (ACS) in Portland, Oregon, to construct a model to determine what they will do tomorrow? The company's flagship product ValueWar is in essence a series of complex algorithms that tries to predict a target's behavior in a certain market. "Some are very simple and are expressed in just a few Greek-like characters," says Mark Chussil, who coded the software. "One very simple algorithm is profit equals revenue minus costs. Others, like calculating demand for a company's product, require pages and pages of densely packed code." Since no one can know what the future holds, ACS lets clients come up with dozens of what-ifs. If a recession depresses demand, competitors slash prices, or if a better competing product comes out of nowhere, an ACS client can have a response plan in place.

Do these tools violate SCIP ethical rules? With the exception of Chussil's palmist algorithms and Raytheon's Silent Runner, yes.

But so do many members of SCIP, and so does much of corporate America. And there is no way to stop them.

2

Motorola:
First in Business Collection

While the Soviets were successfully siphoning off much of America's R&D for its military, heads were hanging low at one of its top targets: Motorola, the multibillion-dollar electronics and semiconductor concern out of Schaumburg, Illinois. It was 1985 and the economy was fueled by massive government deficits and floating skyward on a stock bubble. President Ronald Reagan was two-thirds through his second term, cell phones were strictly viewed as toys for the rich, physicist Timothy Berners-Lee had yet to conceive the protocols that would one day make possible the World Wide Web, and Motorola was losing a frantic bidding war for Storno A/S, a European maker of land-mobile radio systems.

General Electric had purchased Storno a decade earlier for $10 million but was shedding the company to further CEO Jack Welch's radical new approach: concentrating on industries in which it could be number one or two, and jettisoning the rest—a strategy that would ultimately prove highly successful. Bidders were a global who's who of vicious competitors, including techno-Godzilla NEC of Japan, phone maker Ericcson, and German über-giants Siemens, Bosch, and Mannheim, as well as companies from France and the United States.

With sales edging up toward $100 million, Storno was a prized jewel for a number of reasons. It had an excellent reputation for high-quality radio systems and equipped a number of European police forces and militaries. The Copenhagen-based firm, which had 1,800 employees and plants in Denmark, West Germany, and England, maintained strong ties with deep-pocketed customers, and the company that could nab it had the potential to become a dominant player in a fragmented European market. Motorola had only a 20 percent share of the mobile communications at that time and figured it could push it to 60 percent in no time by grabbing Storno. Unfortunately, Motorola was not having much success with the bidding and knew it was going to lose.

But then a Motorola analyst spotted a one-line blurb in a financial newsletter that reported that negotiations between GE and front-runner Bosch had broken down—and that's when Jan Herring was called in. Two years earlier Herring had been lured away from the CIA to develop the first corporate intelligence division in the United States. The man behind the hiring: Motorola's then-CEO Robert W. Galvin, who had served on the president's Foreign Intelligence Advisory Board in the early 1970s. From that experience, Galvin learned that foreign intelligence agencies routinely spied on American corporations and passed on key technical information to their industries.

CEO since 1959, the ferrous-willed Galvin began his career at Motorola in 1940, the year before America enlisted in World War II, and would remain at the helm until 1990, when he took a job as chairman of Motorola's executive committee. Galvin, who inherited the CEO job from his father, was a worthy heir to the throne. He was a do-it-yourselfer who had taught himself how to slice silicon wafers (so he would have a better understanding of the company's technology) and who found no greater joy than climbing up a tree and hacking off branches with a chainsaw. A hands-on leader, many days he took lunch in the corporate cafeteria. His three-decade tenure as CEO of Motorola lasted through eight presidents, four recessions, the atmosphere-shattering launches of *Sputnik* and *Apollo 11*, the height of the Cold War to its ignominious end, and sweeping changes in the global business landscape. It is even more remarkable, given the fact Motorola was a technology company that, to stay ahead of the competition, had to constantly reinvent itself and its technologies. "One of the things we try to do is put ourselves out of business," Galvin once boasted. "That's the most dramatic renewal you can have."

His fear, however, was that state-sponsored intelligence agencies—and not just those working for enemies like the Soviet bloc and China, but also allies like France, Israel, and Japan—were pilfering secrets from Motorola, giving rival industries abroad an edge. It was no coincidence that Japanese companies would end up driving Motorola out of the radio and TV business and leapfrogging its semiconductor technology in both speed and reliability, while Israel would go on to develop one of the world's hottest tech sectors. The French company Thomson was founding its semiconductor industry on pilfered Motorola technology.

But being aware of the threat of espionage and convincing Galvin's subordinates at Motorola to back him were two entirely different things. When Galvin first broached the idea of a division dedicated to gathering intelligence, company bean counters balked. At a megacorporation like Motorola, anything that didn't increase the bottom line and relate directly to selling a phone, microchip, or automobile part was viewed as overhead, which was traditionally kept as low as possible. Division managers were given broad powers to make their numbers and held accountable if they didn't.

Galvin knew he couldn't force the issue by issuing a royal edict. Without true acceptance, however, the program would fail. You can't dictate people's loyalties. If he tried to, the business intelligence unit would surely be shunted aside and never used. When Galvin began discussions with the different divisions, three held varying levels of interest and two wanted no part. The one with the keenest desire to work with a business intelligence unit was the semiconductor division, the one that had been victimized the most, watching helplessly as some of its R&D ended up in the hands of rivals.

Galvin also believed Motorola's fundamental understanding of strategy was fatally flawed. He complained that some people working for him threw the word around only because it sounded important and made their statements sound authoritative. "My strategy is to be number one," they'd say, but their idea of strategy, he joked, was figuring out what to order at lunch. His definition was "the timely and effective application of resources" that "provides a benefit to Motorola customers its competitors can't match," or if they can, not profitably or quickly enough. But it requires vast amounts of information to create a coherent strategy. The company may have succeeded on the merits of its engineers, accountants, salespeople, and technicians, but it would survive by formulating strategy based on a true understanding of the economic and technological landscape.

It was a series of setbacks in the late 1970s and early 1980s that gave the company the impetus it needed to make Galvin's dream of an in-house intelligence-gathering apparatus a reality. In 1979, Motorola earnings were depressed largely because the company had underestimated the intense demand for its microprocessors by electronic games makers. Led by Mattel, which two years earlier scored first with a $10 electronic game called "Blip," Coleco, Milton Bradley, and some thirty other companies jumped chip-first into the then-burgeoning $300 million market, deemphasizing their traditional toy businesses in the process. Motorola couldn't keep up with demand and its earnings, as well as those of its competitors, flattened out at a time they should have been soaring. Then Motorola handed over almost the entire American automobile semiconductor market to the Japanese when the Big Three— Ford, GM, and Chrysler—forced to clean up their act and install catalytic converters, lost patience with American chip makers. Motorola vastly underestimated Detroit's resolve in staring down the American microprocessor industry in requiring chips that would be essentially foolproof but could exist in a gritty, hostile engine environment. As a result, Detroit started buying microprocessors stamped "Made in Japan."

Perhaps the company's biggest avoidable folly was its stubborn insistence in the late 1970s that citizens band radios were here to stay, a fad already on the wane. Motorola, again misreading Detroit, fully expected it would make a killing over the universal installation of CB radios as standard equipment in American cars. Detroit essentially said "10-4, roger out" to that idea, and Motorola's finance sheet became weighed down with a glut in supply. A little business intelligence could have saved the company millions and perhaps helped to prevent Japan, which was absolutely despised in Detroit for whipping American car makers in its core expertise, from gaining a foothold in the emerging auto-chip market.

Now that Galvin had successfully convinced his company into at least accepting, although not quite yet embracing, the existence of a CI division within Motorola, he needed someone to create it. He realized he didn't require someone with a Harvard MBA or extensive business experience, a guy good at numbers, margins, or making sales. It took professionals to provide national security intelligence for the government, he reasoned, and it would take professionals to do the job for big business. He needed to do what foreign intelligence agencies were doing. For that, he needed someone with the proper set of skills and experience. So Galvin hired the CIA. More accurately, a star player within the agency: Jan Herring, a former marine with one of those names that so perfectly describe the work of a CIA agent, who came equipped with an extensive background in government-sponsored business intelligence.

If there is one word that describes Herring, it would be adaptable. He says that when he peers into a mirror he sees someone "pretty damn average and not overly athletic, even though I was in the Marine Corps." In fact, it's almost as if Herring had a charisma bypass operation, which is the way he likes it. Born around the start of World War II, about the time Galvin started work at Motorola, Herring was a Missouri man, a union meat cutter from the age of sixteen to twenty-five, except for the three years he was in the service. For a while he paid his way through college—he earned a bachelor's in physics from the University of Missouri—by working days at the meathouse and nights at the nearby state asylum (or "the funny farm," as he calls it). He also taught math at a girls' high school. Herring joined the CIA in 1963 and rose rapidly through the ranks. He gathered data for trade representatives hammering out GATT, supported the Commerce Department in negotiations with Japan and China, and supplied information to the Treasury Department on the world oil situation in the early 1980s. Herring also managed the department overseeing the Strategic Arms Limitation Talks (SALT).

Known within the CIA as a highly capable intelligence officer and a stickler for rules, Herring seemed perfect for the job at Motorola.

He wasn't the only one considered for the post. Galvin's chief of staff spent a year searching for the ideal candidate, interviewing a dozen men: engineers, businessmen, State Department officials, and agents from military intelligence and the CIA. But it was nearly impossible to find someone with a profound understanding of intelligence, technology, and the private sector. Eventually Galvin's chief of staff offered the job to Tim Stone, an analyst working under Herring whose job was to assess technology, primarily aerospace and electronics. But Stone received a presidential fellowship that enabled him to take a year off to work in the private sector. He would end up working at Motorola all right, but in the semiconductor division. Creating a CIA-like clone was not part of the terms of the grant. So Stone recommended his boss.

At first Herring had to demur. He was running a Reagan-initiated project called the Technology Transfer Assessment Center (TTAC). His job was to detect and prevent the Soviet bloc from stealing American technology. Herring believed deeply in what he was doing and as an added bonus was totally in his element, gathering intelligence and briefing allies on the Soviet threat to Western technology.

By now Galvin was getting antsy, and told his staff if they couldn't find someone, he would. Motorola came back to Herring, offering him the chance to leave his imprint on corporate America, not to mention a huge bump up in salary from what he was earning at the agency. At the time, there was an ongoing debate within the CIA on whether the agency should do what the other intelligence agencies around the world were doing—collecting intelligence on foreign industry and passing it on to their own corporations—or remain committed to its traditional mission of national security. Herring wanted to share intelligence with American business and was extremely critical of the policy that prevented this; some of his former colleagues portray him as "outspoken" on the issue.

The CIA, however, changes for no man. Herring had been with the agency twenty years, much of it analyzing the private sector. He also recognized a potent market for private-sector intelligence operations. Now, he thought, he would get to apply what he had learned. One thing that impressed Galvin about his hireling-to-be was that they shared many of the same conclusions. "My last ten years in government service I saw that not just the Chinese and Russians, but also our allies—the French, Israelis, and Japanese—were gathering intelligence on American companies to benefit their businesses," Herring says. "The competition had been shifting from issues of national security to issues of national economics. These governments were looking out for their businesses." By law the CIA was not allowed to follow suit, but Herring believed companies could do it for themselves. He figured it would take him about three years to get a CI division fully up and running within Motorola, ten years for the business culture to completely embrace and make proper use of it. A patient man who knew what he wanted, Galvin told Herring he would report directly to him, wiping away potential bureaucratic hurdles.

Herring says the thing that scared him most about his new job was that in the government he had thousands of agents collecting information and hundreds supporting him in his analytic role. At Motorola he had ten people, five of them he would train as analysts, yet he would have to somehow marshal company resources to mimic the basic functions of the government. At the CIA there were 100 librarians, at Motorola a small library and a lone librarian. But the CIA wasn't just about cloak-and-dagger spy ops. Herring knew from experience it relied extensively on publicly available information that was not classified—newspaper and magazine articles, books, newsletters, tips, academic studies and papers, research carried out by the U.S. Commerce Department, and local chambers of commerce. This, he says, covers 90 percent of the information the CIA gathers.

He figured he could create the equivalent of 200 government librarians with one Motorola librarian, a computer, and an electronic mail system, an almost unheard-of theory in the days before the wide deployment of e-mail, instant messaging, and web sites. Even in the early 1980s, Motorola had its own communications network, and it relied heavily on faxes and telexes. Herring also had 90,000 employees at his disposal, if he could figure out a way to get them involved. He decided to create small networks of teams with specific responsibilities and, when he had to, tap the brainpower within the company. "In this way," he says, "we were emulating the government's three-pronged operational functions model: information, human source intelligence, and analysis."

His first days on the job were spent getting to know the attorney who had been assigned to him full-time. So new was the concept of an in-house intelligence gathering apparatus that no one quite knew what types of legal and ethical guidelines policies should be put in place. Galvin and Herring agreed that if Motorola was to succeed in this radical notion of a business intelligence system, it would have to be completely aboveboard. Anyone working for Herring was required to begin every phone call by identifying himself as a Motorola employee, as in "I am with Motorola's Business Intelligence Department." Herring wanted to call the unit the Office of Analytical Research, afraid no one would talk to them if they identified themselves as working in business intelligence. But Galvin said he wanted to make the point that "intelligence is an honorable profession" and should be treated as such. No scams, no social engineering, no front companies, no stealing, no blackmail, no wire taps, no posing as something you weren't.

The 1970s and early 1980s were a period when the agency was under intense fire in the press and in Congress for shielding a "rogue element," a place where assassinations were allegedly planned and carried out: the assassination of Allende in Chile, the sabotaging of Nicaragua's ports, Iran/contra, and arms for hostages. The last thing Herring says he wanted was for some investigative journalist to splash his name on the front page for do-

ing something unethical. "The minute you do something illegal
you put the whole company in legal jeopardy."

Herring spent the rest of his inception phase looking for help,
going on a hiring campaign, and taking on three men over the age
of fifty-five, all of whom had strong backgrounds in technology.
One had worked for GE as a transportation expert, the other assisted McDonnell Douglas in setting up factories, and the third
had been a chemical and energy-technology consultant for Arthur
D. Little.

Herring started off spending a lot of time on the road, teaching
employees Corporate Intelligence Gathering 101. He explained
what to look for, ways to get it, and how to prevent competitors
from snatching information from Motorola. He trained a cadre of
managers so they could do their own intelligence. Who else, he
reasoned, would know what they needed and how to crunch the
data better than those with an intimate understanding of Motorola's technology, their markets, and their competitors?

Galvin told him about the initial resistance to setting up a business intelligence unit and advised Herring to reach out to the divisions with the greatest interest and need. As a result, Herring was
able to develop a number of loyal contacts within the semiconductor and automotive sections—underachieving divisions under pressure to add more to the company's bottom line—who were only
too glad to work with him to improve their fortunes.

By the time the bidding for Storno was under way, Herring had
taught dozens of key Motorola employees in the States and
abroad methods in collecting information and what to do with it
once they had it. If they weren't sure, they could always pass raw
data directly to Herring and his staff, which acted as a clearing-
house for intelligence.

Herring had traveled all over the Motorola world, to Japan, Europe, and the Far East, logging tens of thousands of miles in the

process, introducing himself to the managers and engineers who would either make or break his program. He showed them tricks on how to informally chat up sources for information without misrepresenting who they were; the key is to ensure that the target doesn't know he's providing key intelligence. He pointed them to grossly underutilized resources, like American embassies abroad with vast libraries of Commerce Department studies. He taught them how to read between the lines of a foreign newspaper and how to interview targets working at Motorola's competitors. These were people on the bottom rung of the corporate ladder, blue-collar types who often felt underappreciated and were more than happy to inform on their employer. He instructed Motorola managers to hire outside newsletter editors to create special detailed editions for Motorola, because they rarely publish everything they know.

Even the tiniest speck of information could lead to a windfall. The trick was to be diligent about collecting it. In his dealings with company employees, Herring's understated personality worked to his advantage. People whose impressions of CIA agents were right out of Robert Ludlum pulp novels and James Bond flicks were surprised to meet a diligent, respectful, quiet man who believed passionately in toeing the ethical line. In the CIA, failure is often not an acceptable option. At Motorola, failure would be tolerated as long as the company's business intelligence guidelines were not breached.

But now came his first true test: Storno. By the time his analyst had come across the newsletter blurb that set the whole process in motion, Herring had all the pieces he needed in place and was eager to justify Galvin's confidence in him. The first thing Herring did was send out a companywide APB. Sure, he might have only ten people working directly under him, and another twenty who contributed to his unit, but he had the entire Motorola empire to draw on, a veritable wave of human assets, many of whom he had come across in his travels.

The key question was why did negotiations between GE and Bosch falter? For Motorola to take the lead in the siutuation, the company would need to know. Who pulled out of the negotiations, GE or Bosch? What was the deal-breaker–a disagreement over money, or did European regulators put the kibosh on an agreement? Were there legal squabbles? A personality conflict among negotiators? Did Danish Storno executives kick up a fuss, wary of working for Germans, whom many Danes have still not forgiven for World War II? Or was it the quasi-socialist Danish government that scotched the agreement? Was Storno fearful of being broken up and stripped of its technology by a ruthless competitor? Did German politicians sabotage the sale? Any of these problems could have scuttled the deal.

Awaiting a response from his Motorola virtual army division, Herring and his team worked the phones, calling various financial analysts and the publisher of the newsletter. The analyst who wrote the one-line blurb about the trouble GE had sealing the deal told Herring that Bosch was stuck on one position, but he didn't know which. But it was one of Herring's human assets who really came through. Within hours a Motorola executive responsible for managing the company's activities in France called Herring. He had a treasure trove of business and government contacts within France and Germany and had discovered the Storno deal had fallen through because of a disagreement over the company's value.

Herring asked him to keep working his personal network. The man quickly discovered that Bosch had drawn a line in the sand: "They had made their best offer and wouldn't back down," Herring recalls. Motorola's country manager for France also reported the French company was not all that interested in acquiring Storno, and Ericcson seemed clueless, giving him the impression the

Swedish phone maker didn't understand what was at stake. As for NEC, employees working for Motorola's Japanese branch got the skinny by simply by going out for drinks with representatives from NEC. They elicited the fact that NEC was having trouble communicating with GE. Japan's business culture, which emphasizes personal relationships and after-hours carousing to engender "wa," or harmony, was in stark contrast to GE's lean and mean business machine.

Herring concluded that with the right offer, Storno could be Motorola's. He quickly put together an "IR," a one-page intelligence report—one of the staples of good competitor intelligence work. The report consisted of a two-sentence summary of the situation, why the acquisition of Storno was important for the well-being of the company, and four paragraphs outlining the facts as he knew them. Herring sent it to CEO Galvin, the company's vice chairman, the head of the communications division, who had been in charge of the initial bid for Storno, the vice president of acquisitions, and the chief financial officer. The vice president of acquisitions put together a package and flew to GE's headquarters in New York with his colleague from the communications division, and within a week of Herring sending the memo, Motorola had what it wanted all along.

Motorola and GE signed an agreement in principle for the sale of Storno in January 1986, and the acquisition was closed three months later. The price Motorola paid GE for Storno remains a tightly held secret to this day, but an SEC filing made by GE for fiscal 1986 mentions "unusual gains in 1986" that "arose from the sale of a small foreign affiliate ($12 million) and adjustments to previous unusual disposition provisions ($38 million)"—for a total of $50 million. Not a bad investment. Motorola/Storno's mobile-phone plant in Flensburg is now the most productive of Motorola's six such plants worldwide and Motorola maintains a strong presence on the Continent. Perhaps even more important to Herring, this event proved the power of corporate-sponsored business intelligence.

But Storno wasn't the only success Herring and his intelligence unit had at Motorola. That same year, Motorola was intent on spreading farther into Japan. But, as Galvin likes to point out, much of business negotiation on a global level occurs among groups of people who have far different cultures, belief systems, customs, and ways of conducting business. Ignorance of these differences can lead, as NEC and GE discovered, to stalled negotiations. Motorola was already fairly big in Japan, although it wasn't as profitable a market as the company would have liked. Still, it knew it had to maintain a strong presence there. It decided the best strategy would be to either acquire a Japanese company or form a partnership. Motorola narrowed its choices down to three companies. Two of them were Japanese trading partners of Motorola, the other was Toshiba, a competitor. On the face of it negotiating a deal with the trading partners would seem to offer the path of least resistance.

Herring and his staff got down to work and studied the Japanese distribution system, an intricate network of sellers and resellers that is a prime reason for the nation's high price levels, as well as a significant barrier to American companies selling their wares in Japan. With so many tiny mom-and-pop stores (no malls at the time), each dependent on the goodwill of a major Japanese manufacturer, companies without an in to the network found themselves out of luck. Motorola decided the best way to succeed in Japan would be to align itself with a major Japanese company that could push its products through this intricate value-added maze. Now that it knew what it wanted, Motorola had to figure out how to get it.

Herring studied the three Japanese companies, detailing their businesses and corporate culture. "Sixty percent of mergers and acquisitions fail, especially those among companies in different countries, and not because the business deal wasn't good," Herring says. "It's the nonbusiness attributes, often mere personality clashes and differences in corporate culture, that can cause major problems."

Motorola's CEO, president, and other executives would be the ones to meet with each of these companies. The question was, would they get along? Herring was not interested in the business of the deal; that was outside the scope of his duties. He wanted to know about each of the companies' management cultures. The Japanese are primarily Shinto and Buddhist. Would that cause a clash? Would they protect Motorola intellectual property? Herring knew a good person to contact first would be Tom Irie, a former NEC executive who was the head of Motorola Japan. He asked Irie to make discreet inquiries about each of the companies. Are they easy to work with? Do they keep their word? Can they be trusted? Does anti-American sentiment run deep? How have their partnerships with foreign firms worked out? Herring also had his team work their contacts at other American corporations and the commercial, economic, and scientific attachés at the American Embassy in Japan.

Over time, a murky picture began to clear up. The two Japanese firms with which Motorola had already forged trading partnerships maintained a traditional Japanese business culture. Their leaders were Shinto and did not respond to American gregariousness. They maintained rigid cultural barriers and a direct connection to their religious and cultural roots, and Western companies did not report positive interactions. Some even claimed the two companies had failed to live up to their obligations, hiding behind an impenetrable cloak. Herring surmised that meant they put their company and country above all else, and it would not be easy for Motorola to strike a deal, one that would require both companies to establish a mutual bond of trust.

At the same time, the information coming in about Toshiba was more promising. The Japanese electronics maker was desperate for semiconductor technology, something Motorola had in spades: This gave Motorola the leverage it required to strike a hard bargain. Galvin's experiences with Motorola in Japan had brought him to the realization that the Japanese respect power, "in contrast to the differential polite mannerisms of the more apparent culture." Later on, Galvin would make good use of this knowledge, using every ounce of political power Motorola could muster to pry open Japan's electronics market, from calling in the Senate Foreign Relations Committee to getting Presidents Reagan and Bush to push the point. "The Japanese respected us for it and responded by purchasing our products," Galvin concluded. "They respected power. That's an anthropological principle, and a very significant piece of intelligence."

But having something Toshiba wanted wouldn't be enough. Herring needed to know more about Toshiba, especially its behavior in prior business arrangements with American firms. He contacted Ampex, a pioneer in videotape and data storage, which had entered into a joint venture with Toshiba that ultimately failed. Amazingly, company managers reported that the failure wasn't owing to anything Toshiba had done. In fact, Toshiba honored the agreement beyond the point Apex could contribute anything significant because Toshiba felt an obligation to keep its word. After Galvin was briefed on this, he gave the go-ahead to initiate negotiations. But this didn't mean Herring was done.

While Motorola made friendly overtures to Toshiba about a potential deal, Herring crafted personality profiles of each member of Toshiba's negotiating team. He based them roughly on a form of the Myers-Briggs Type Indicator, a psychological profiling tool used to predict human behavior. The beauty of it was you didn't need to be a psychologist to administer it, which is why it is still the most popular personality test in business intelligence in the world. Translated into twenty languages and taken by more than two million people a year, it was first developed in the 1940s as a screening and selection tool. In the 1980s, corporations began using it to test potential employees. But Herring, basing his theories on those of John Nolan, a former government intelligence collector who had retooled the test for the business world, knew it offered rich potential.

Of course, as Nolan has pointed out, you're not going to get an unsuspecting target from a rival corporation to sit down with a number two pencil and fill out a detailed questionnaire with some 120 questions. That meant Herring would have to develop both the questions and, through hard-nosed research, the answers, too. For someone like him, who synthesized thousands of pages of intelligence when at the CIA, Herring knew he could get just as accurate an assessment of his targets without ever saying a word to them. He admits his test, which he dubs "an expanded who's who," was primitive (it would take Nolan to later perfect Briggs-Myers for use in CI), but it was effective nevertheless.

Nowadays such personality profiles are popular among business intelligence professionals. As Jonathan Calof, a consultant and professor at the University of Ottawa, says, corporate decisions are ultimately made by people, and human nature tends to make us react similarly in similar circumstances. "If I know your chief executive used to be in marketing or R&D or in finance, I may get a sense of how he sees the world," Calof says. "And I can look at previous decisions he's made," both for his present company and for his previous employer. But during Herring's time at Motorola, even the concept of business intelligence was practically unknown, let alone reliance on personality tests.

Herring had Motorola's Tom Irie, formerly of Toshiba Japan, hire a Japanese law firm to check up on Toshiba. The firm, headquartered in Tokyo, contacted someone who knew one of the Toshiba executives and paid him to take the unwitting source to dinner and drinks. The contact asked the Toshiba executive what he thought of his job and his views on the company's president, vice president, and anyone else who could potentially be part of Toshiba's negotiating team. He inquired about Toshiba's corporate culture, its business dealings, successes and failures, the educational background of key personnel, and whether anyone had trained and lived in the United States—all under the guise a friendly business gossip, without the Toshiba executive knowing it was Motorola that was ultimately taking notes.

Meanwhile, Herring kept working corporate contacts in the United States. One of his staff located a manager at GE who had gone sailing with a Toshiba executive and hit him up for information. Herring and his contact reached out to people who had gone to school with Toshiba executives, their friends, acquaintances, and business rivals. "By the time we were through," Herring says, "we had a pretty complete history of our counterparts. One of the most attractive things about potentially working with Toshiba was the fact that one of its senior executives was Christian, which surprised us. This implied the company was more open, less rigid, and more accepting to Western ideals." Most Japanese companies put great stock in their employees' family backgrounds, and those without the proper pedigree usually found their careers stalled in midstream. Performance took a backseat to stultifying rules of conduct. If you didn't fit in, prove your loyalty to the company by endless socializing after work with the members of your department, you weren't fired. Instead, you could end up even worse: "madogi wa zoku," or the man by the window, twiddling away your days, worthless and disrespected by your peers. In a culture that emphasizes the group, this was the equivalent of purgatory. Since Toshiba had accepted someone with a different religion in its ruling ranks,

Toshiba didn't have a typical conservative corporate culture. Motorola representatives, Herring believed, would feel more of a cultural connection with it, which would help any potential deal making go smoother.

As he had with GATT and SALT negotiators during his days with the CIA, Herring provided Motorola deal makers with information—and anecdote-laden personality profiles. Motorola representatives, knowing all about their counterparts across the table—their likes, dislikes, interests, education, hobbies, family background, and prior strategies in corporate negotiations—were able to make breezy conversation; everyone was at ease, and a deal was struck quickly.

"Ironically, competitor intelligence helped deter paranoia," Herring says. "Usually spying breeds paranoia." Afterward, one of Motorola's representatives, so impressed with the profiles, showed one of the dossiers to his Toshiba counterpart, much to Herring's chagrin. But the Toshiba executive took it well. After all, how could he complain? Japanese companies had been spying on American business since the 1950s. The Land of the Rising Sun had played an aggressive game of technological catch-up with the West until the 1980s but was way ahead on business intelligence.

Just because an environment of conviviality and trust had been achieved, however, didn't mean that Motorola, a stern critic of Japanese chip tactics in the past, didn't take a hardened position. Because the company knew about Toshiba's desperate desire for access to Motorola's microprocessor technology, it agreed to pass on its know-how in stages, directly in proportion to Toshiba opening up its distribution system to Motorola, and there would be benchmarks, real numbers that would have to be achieved.

Because of this deal, Galvin had accomplished what no other U.S. company had been able to do previously: crack the Japanese market. At a time of strained trade relations with Japan, he became a hero to corporate America. In fact, Westinghouse Electric Corp. CEO John C. Marous, in a 1988 *Forbes* magazine article, named Galvin his most admired business leader, "for bringing about what success we've achieved in the semiconductor industry between the U.S. and Japan." But Galvin couldn't have done it without Herring.

The coups Motorola scored with Storno and Toshiba made it clear to the corporation's rank and file that Galvin had been right about the value of intelligence. They had already changed the fortunes of the company, which had been reeling only a few years earlier, struggling to find itself in a shifting business climate. It appeared Motorola had found a way to avoid making massive strategic blunders of the type that had depressed its earnings in the late 1970s. Herring and his team, with its paltry $1 million-a-year budget, had, in twenty-four months, contributed 100 times that amount to the bottom line, creating new global opportunities for the company and promising even greater rewards down the road. This created a synergy within the company. Motorola personnel, now that they could see a tangible benefit, embraced Herring's team.

Instead of Motorola's CI division being viewed as the monument that Bob Galvin built, section chiefs began consulting with Herring before beginning business ventures. Word spread throughout the corporate world, a gossipy clique if there ever was one. (Besides, it wasn't as if Galvin and Herring were trying to keep the existence of its business intelligence unit a secret.) Kodak and Ford came calling, and Herring advised them on ways to create their own intelligence units. Then came Alcoa, Pfizer, and 3M, all, in whole or in part, modeling their business intelligence departments after Motorola's. "So many companies were coming through it became a pain," Herring says. "We were spending [so] much time talking to them that it began to cut into our own work."

Corporate America knew a good thing when it saw it, and it didn't take long for other large business concerns to create business intelligence departments: Coca-Cola, Microsoft, General Electric, Intel, Procter & Gamble, and Hewlett-Packard, among others. If Apple, the joke goes, had gotten into competitive intelligence in a timely fashion, the company would have had to bail out Microsoft, instead of the other way around. But it was Herring who had started it all. In 1986, three years after he had invented the genre, Herring helped to found the Society of Competitive Intelligence Professionals, an organization that started out with 150 members. By 2000 membership had swelled to more than 7,000, with three-quarters of the members working at corporations, the rest for consulting firms.

You won't find out how CI departments are funded, though. Just because CI's practitioners pine to come in from the cold, corporations are still afraid to be connected in any way with it. It's bad PR. So companies try to hide it. They do it in ways as cloak and dagger as many of the former government intelligence agents they approach to run their operations. Take a look at the business cards of some SCIP members, which tell you nothing and everything at the same time: "Director of Market Research," "Director of Market Information," "Information Security Consultant," and "Strategic Planning Department." Comb through corporate budgets and you won't find "Spy Section" listed under "Business Intelligence," you'll note a similar vague lexicon, divisions subsumed under innocuous-sounding (although somewhat aptly descriptive) categories like community relations, corporate development, marketing, and research and analysis.

Herring himself, after he left Motorola and moved into his new consultant's role, helped construct business intelligence departments for more American brand-name icons: American Express, Bristol-Myers Squibb, Exxon, IBM, Monsanto, Nutrasweet, and Southwestern Bell. But that doesn't mean his handiwork always survived the vicissitudes of corporate politics.

Of the two dozen CI divisions he helped establish, about half ended up shutting down. Herring constructed an intricate CI division for General Dynamics, but when the company changed its business model from one emphasizing global growth to one of consolidation, it started to sell off its defense industries, and "you don't need much intelligence to further a selling-off strategy," Herring says. Another CI unit he created for Phillips Petroleum suffered a similar fate, but for a different reason. Motorola's business intelligence section succeeded because Galvin gave Herring unrelenting support, but the same couldn't be said of Phillips's CEO. Without leadership from the top, the division was pushed down the command structure, until it fizzled. Contrast that with Motorola, which by 1986 was integrating its business intelligence section into its global strategy, which was what Galvin had planned all along.

Equally important to gathering information is how a company deploys what it learns. "Once all the information has been collected, dissected, and analyzed, it's out of my hands," Herring says. In 1985 he recalls being summoned to the office of the vice chairman, who wanted to know if Motorola's competitors were thinking of using satellite antennae in space to support global communications. Herring and his team performed patent and scientific literature searches, digging for evidence of satellite-based antennae. They noted that the U.S. government, AT&T, and Motorola had filed patents, with Motorola in the lead. By wading through more research they were able to piece together a patchwork of existing technology—a satellite in space outfitted with an antenna that could be retrofitted from fire trucks, communications systems that were deployed by taxi dispatchers—that could be combined to create a space-based communications network. Herring then primed the people responsible for Motorola working with the government and identified two foreign entities with plans to launch communications satellites. Although Herring hadn't come across any evidence that Motorola rivals such as Siemens and Ericcson were plotting the same path, the more satellites being launched, the greater the potential for cutthroat competition, although he calculated this could take them ten years to accomplish.

Herring turned in his findings to Motorola's vice chairman. "I thought he'd be pleased," Herring says, "but he wasn't. He wanted to know, if they were to push it, how fast could they get those satellites up. I told him, if the governments and companies really got behind the project, it could be accomplished in as few as five years." All this would later turn out to be Iridium, a Motorola initiative that would start out with great promise but would eventually crash and burn with the advent of the cellular craze—a technology that offered lighter, more compact phones and cheaper access, costing the company $6 billion.

By 1987, Herring had accomplished what he had set out to do and hired a replacement, his old underling at the CIA, Tim Stone. Herring now has his own consulting company, Herring & Associates, based in Hartford, Connecticut, where he advises brand-name companies on intelligence strategies. He is one of many hundreds of former government agents working in the private sector. But he was the first to be lured over to corporate America and helped found a billion-dollar industry. After he left, Motorola's fortunes continued to improve until the mid-1990s, when a series of missteps caused the company to falter. It missed out on the digital cell phone market, clinging to analog technology, it mistimed expansion into the memory-chip business, and its Iridium project imploded when it couldn't attract enough customers willing to pay exorbitant rates so they could call someone from the middle of the Gobi Desert.

After Bob Galvin stepped down in 1990, Motorola went through two changes in leadership. The company was reeling from poor morale, infighting, and poor strategic decision making. In 1997 the board tapped Bob Galvin's son, Chris, to take the helm, and after a shaky start, the company's fortunes one-eightied within thirty-six months, its stock shooting up ninety points in a year, from $67.75 to $161.375.

What does the younger Galvin attribute much of his success to? The program Herring created: "The reorganization of the [entire Motorola communications] enterprise was partly aided by the intelligence effort, as is our selecting new partners, such as Cisco," he says. "Tactically, we have many examples of market successes." As a result, Galvin was chosen to receive the 1999 Intelligence-Savvy CEO Award for Leadership in Competitive Intelligence. Galvin was selected because of his open support of competitive intelligence practices within Motorola, encouragement of "intelligence standards" like staff training and ethical guidelines, and his freeing up of monies for speeding the flow of critical competitive information.

Like father, like son.

3

The Mole—Victor Lee

About the time Motorola was making its late 1990s comeback under Chris Galvin, some high-ranking Avery Dennison executives realized they had a serious problem.

It was a raw midwestern day in early January 1997, and Victor Lee, a polymer physicist at Avery Fasson Roll Division in Concord, Ohio, was in a meeting about expanding Avery's business into Asia. For Lee, this was particularly career-affirming, since his company, one of the largest adhesives companies in the world, coveted the Asian market (especially China). With almost $4 billion in annual sales, Avery believed that once it got a foothold in Asia it could easily reap double-digit growth rates. Its products were already ubiquitous in offices in the United States and Europe, but Taiwan, China, Hong Kong, Singapore, Korea, Thailand, Malaysia, Indonesia, and the Philippines were a different story. Although Avery manufactured half of the labels sold worldwide, less than 1 percent of those sales came from Asia, excluding Japan and Australia.

Lee was taking mental notes as Avery executive Thomas Allen briefed him and his teammates—his supervisor Prem Krish and Avery colleague Kyung Min—on "important" and "confidential" material contained in a binder. Inside was a packet of information on Avery's factory in India and a memorandum that detailed plans for expanding into the Asian market, stamped "CONFI-DENTIAL" and "For Internal Eyes Only." Allen handed the binder to Krish, whose office they were meeting in, and emphasized the importance of the material to Avery, particularly the memo. The consequences could be dire for Avery if the contents were to find their way to a competitor.

Allen went to great lengths to make sure everybody in the meeting understood that it was "proprietary, confidential information to Avery Dennison" and that Avery was taking the security threat so seriously there would be only one copy of the memo, which would be filed in Prem Krish's office. Allen reminded the group that only he and Krish had clearance to see the memo. If Lee wanted access, he would have to go through his supervisor. Just before the meeting ended Krish, in full view of all the other members of the "international support group," placed the binder in his filing cabinet and announced he would be taking a vacation.

Greed clouding common sense, Lee didn't wait for Krish to call a cab to the airport before returning to his supervisor's empty office fifteen minutes later. Lee was an expert in a somewhat arcane yet commercially significant area of science called rheology, a science dealing with the flow of matter. His claim to adhesives fame: He had invented a way to measure the force required to peel off a sticky label. But for all his knowledge of academic and commercial esoterica, Lee was a terrible spy. He inspected the room, peered through the window, and shut the blinds.

Satisfied no one had seen him, Lee pulled on a pair of gray winter gloves, opened the file cabinet and leafed through the file. He didn't have time to read the top-secret memo; he just wanted to make sure it was really there. Satisfied it was, Lee put everything back and slipped away.

The next day the camera, standard FBI-issue, caught his stealthy return. This time he made sure to lock the door behind him. He inspected the forbidden document. Included on the first two confidential pages were plans calling for an international support group and a listing of regional competitors as "sources of experienced local talent in Taiwan," including glue makers Four Pillars, Solar, Imei, and KK Converting, all emphasized in bold. The next four pages were dedicated to a new factory in India, complete with diagrams and pictures. Satisfied, Lee left the room (and camera range) for enough time to make photocopies. He then reappeared, putting everything back.

What he didn't know was that Avery had gotten wind of his activities and worked with the Bureau to set him up. Two months later, after subpoenaing Dr. Lee's financial records, getting a court order to put a PEN register on his phones so all outgoing calls could be recorded, and reviewing his telephone call history, federal agents confronted Lee with the evidence. Within three hours he caved in, admitting that for seven years he had been passing "confidential" information to an Avery competitor in Asia, Four Pillars Enterprises of Taiwan. "We were all shocked," sums up executive vice president Kim A. Caldwell, who worked alongside Lee in Avery's Ohio facility.

Avery's nemesis was a mid-size Taiwanese manufacturer of heavy-duty insulation and plumbing tape for sealing ducts, air conditioners, windows, and pipes. The company, with 70 percent of the paper adhesives market in Taiwan and China and sales of about $160 million, sold a wide (and somewhat quirky) array of products, some of which went toe-to-toe with Avery offerings. In addition to the usual repair tapes under its Deer Park brand, Four Pillars catered to a decidedly Chinese consumer appetite in Asia. It offered apothecary staples like "Diet Tape" ("Simply wrap the tape around joints of the fingers and weight loss will occur"), "Acne removal cloth tape"

("The cloth tape touch closely to the skin around nose, then can remove annoying acne and clean dirt and greasy spots"), and the miracle cure "Nasal Cleaning Tape."

For most of their histories, Avery and Four Pillars did not consider themselves competitors. Four Pillars concentrated on selling tape to the Asian market, whereas Avery's business was mostly in sticky labels outside of Asia. For a time, the two companies had even entertained a joint venture to exploit the Asian market together, but Avery backed out. Four Pillars claims it was because Avery was using it to gain access to the tape and label market in mainland China. Avery says the reason was that Four Pillars refused to share key financial information. James D. Robenalt of Thompson Hine & Flory, a lawyer for Avery, says the joint venture talks ended in 1993, when Four Pillars gave Avery Dennison data that suggested it had lost revenues in the tape business, its main source of revenue.

Four Pillars was also trying to get into the computer business, which was not a core business, and it was losing money at that, too. "When Avery made a request for additional financial information, Four Pillars had a fire in one of their facilities," says Robenalt. The company asked for more time. Then it declined to release the data. But Avery had seen enough and decided to end talks. Both sides did turn over commercial samples to each other, Robenalt admits, "but nobody gave anything of any highly confidential nature. They had discussions. They exchanged financials." No formulas changed hands, although he claims "we found them with formulas [from Avery] in their files." By the mid-1990s, instead of teaming up, they were rivals. Avery was jumping headlong into Asia, Four Pillars' turf, and Four Pillars was getting into Avery's bread and butter: labels and stickers.

Twenty times the size of Four Pillars, Avery Dennison was one of the world's 500 biggest corporations. On its web site the company bragged that "whenever you use something that's self-adhesive, there's a good chance Avery Dennison made it. . . . When you go to the grocery store, you'll almost certainly put products bearing Avery Dennison labels into your shopping basket. When you drive home, you'll most likely be surrounded by Avery Dennison self-adhesive products that decorate your car inside and out, and make your dashboard instruments readable. Your trip will be made safer by Avery Dennison reflective products on road signs." The glorified glue maker could have added that every time you seal your IRS form 1040 and send it to the tax man, stanch bleeding with a Band-Aid, or buy hundreds of other products that come equipped with a label—from batteries to clothes to wine—you are probably using an Avery Dennison product. Founded during the Great Depression, the powerful multinational, which calls Pasadena, California, home, also sells self-adhesive labels for personal care, pharmaceuticals, food and beverage products, and even computer peripherals.

As the company pun runs, "Avery Dennison is easy to label." But a better motto might be: We manufacture all the piddly crap you never think about—the millions upon millions of adhesive labels and stamps used on packages and school and office products, such as the trusty HI-LITER, notebooks, three-ring binders, markers, fasteners, business forms, tickets, and tags. In 1935 R. Stanton Avery, working out of a 100-square-foot loft space in Los Angeles, manufactured the world's first self-adhesive labels. His very first product: a little round sticker used to mark prices. By the end of World War II annual sales for Avery Adhesives approached half a million dollars. Nowadays, Avery Dennison has more than 8,000 times that in yearly revenue. It boasts more than 100 manufacturing facilities and employs 15,000 people (2,000 in Ohio, where Lee worked), maintaining sales offices in three dozen countries, selling products in some ninety countries. Nearly 75 percent of the company's business relates to pressure-sensitive adhesive products, which are converted into labels and other goods through die-cutting, embossing, printing, and stamping; others are sold in unconverted form as base materials, tapes, and reflective sheeting. And nowhere is the company more focused then on its home turf.

Victor Lee had been with the multinational adhesives maker for more than a decade, after earning advanced degrees from three American universities, focusing on the field of rheology. His father had died when Lee was three, leaving a wife and four sons (Lee being the youngest). After a childhood of poverty, Lee obtained his B.S. in chemical engineering from Taiwan University in Taipei in 1973, then did his compulsory military service. After a two-year stint in the Taiwanese army he took a job at an artificial fiber plant located in a Taipei suburb, but this lasted only two weeks. He didn't like the work environment and wasn't sure what he wanted to do with his life. In 1976 Lee decided to leave his family and go to graduate school in the United States, where he attended the University of Oklahoma in northern Oklahoma. He earned a master's in chemical engineering in 1978, then transferred to Texas Tech University in Lubbock, Texas, where he met his wife, who is also Taiwanese, and received his Ph.D. Lee's next stop was Kent State University, where he worked as a postdoctoral research fellow, looking into gas/solid absorption, a chemical process in which gas can be deposited on a solid. But not satisfied with the educational equivalent of a trifecta—bachelor's, master's, and Ph.D.—Lee decided to enroll at the University of Akron to study polymer science and ring up another master's degree.

In 1986 Avery Dennison Fasson Roll Division (Fasson is a jumble of the words "fasten" and "on") hired Lee as a staff rheologist at an annual salary of $33,000. He joined some five dozen other scientists on staff. His first assignment was to work on the newly arrived rheometer, a contraption courtesy of the Avery Research Center in Pasadena and used to measure the deformation of an adhesive. Lee was given the assignment of setting up the equipment, learning how to run it, then interpreting the data so Avery could develop pressure-sensitive products for market more quickly.

For the Avery Dennison of the late 1980s and early 1990s, Lee was an important hire. Prior to his arrival, formulating an adhesive at Avery took a lot of trial and error, requiring company chemists and technicians to blindly mix ingredients, hoping to strike adhesives gold, which in many instances took more than two years. The company needed ways to get its products into the marketplace as quickly and as efficiently as possible. Anything that could help the company realize sales faster meant more revenue. Lee helped take some of the guesswork out of creating adhesives, some of which require many layers of chemicals to make a label stick to a surface but not leave a sticky residue. Lee was also responsible for creating another useful test method called "high-speed release," assigning numerical values to the force necessary to peel away a sticker from various surfaces—wood versus metal versus Sheetrock versus plastic. According to Lawrence Mitchell, an Avery executive, Lee became the company's number one expert in high-speed release testing.

Avery characterizes Lee as a "hard-working, bright, and meticulous scientist with attention to detail and thoroughness" who had quickly climbed the Avery ladder to senior research engineer. But Lee never could shake the feeling that it would some day, somehow all be taken away from him. He was plagued by the fear that he would slip back into the type of oppressive poverty he had survived as a child. Since he had used academia as his coach ticket to middle-class America, Lee put great stock in education and fretted over how he would put his daughter, who was born in 1980, through college. By the time she would graduate from high school, he knew that college tuition plus room and board could top $30,000 a year at the best schools, which would be almost half his salary.

Lee's relationship with Four Pillars began in July 1989, when he was taking his first vacation to Taiwan since leaving for the United States sixteen years earlier. Before joining his wife and daughter at his mother-in-law's home in Taipei for a three-week vacation, Lee had received a call from a former Texas Tech classmate, Ta-sheng Wang. When Wang heard Lee would be vacationing in Taiwan, he invited him to present a lecture on pressure-sensitive adhesives to about two dozen people invited by Taiwan's Industrial Research Institute, a semiofficial organization affiliated with the Taiwanese Department of Economics.

Lee was flattered, even more so when Wang, who was a chemical engineer but not familiar with Lee's specialty, polymer science, advised him to "just pick a topic, whatever you are good at." In mid-July 1989 he gave a ninety-minute presentation at the Taiwanese think tank's offices in Hsinchu, Taiwan, using publicly accessible material Lee had got from the annual meeting of the Pressure Sensitive Tape Council. It didn't even occur to him to ask Avery's permission.

One of the lecture guests was a Four Pillars employee, who told a company vice president, C. K. Kao, about Lee's presentation. Kao knew Lee from his postgraduate days at the University of Taiwan, where he had been a teaching assistant for a class Lee had taken as an undergraduate. Remembering his former student, Kao asked him to give the same lecture at Four Pillars. This was Lee's first time back to Taiwan since he'd left, practically penniless, a bachelor's degree in hand, years of academia ahead of him. Now he was being asked by his former instructor to give a presentation? Lee felt flushed with honor and good fortune. It was like being asked by your alma mater to give the graduation address. Within a week of receiving Kao's call, Lee offered the same seminar to about a dozen people at Four Pillars, including Hwei-Chen "Sally" Yang, the daughter of company president P. Y. Yang. Afterward, Lee received the equivalent of $100 for gas and mileage.

A few days later Kao phoned again to say that Four Pillars' president Yang hadn't had the chance to attend Lee's presentation but would like to meet for dinner. Lee joined P. Y. Yang, Kao, Sally Yang, and a couple of Four Pillars engineers at a local restaurant. Lee, the guest of honor, sat next to company president Yang. After chatting for a couple of hours, getting to know each other, Lee, Kao, and both Yangs repaired to a coffee parlor, where they broke up into two groups: P. Y. and Lee sat at one table; Sally and Kao at another a few yards away. P. Y. Yang took Lee into his confidence, telling the Avery scientist he would like Four Pillars to strengthen its label business. It was fine in tape, Yang confided, but labels were different. Maybe Lee could teach them what he knew. Lee told him "honestly that I have very limited industrial experience, so probably there is not much I can teach." Yang persisted, however, saying it didn't matter. "Just teach whatever you know you can teach us."

He offered Lee $25,000 in U.S. currency for the first year of consulting, which, since Lee was making $45,000 at the time, was more than half his annual salary, plus additional periodic payments of between $10,000 and $15,000. There was, however, one caveat: "No one needs to know about this," Yang said. He would keep Lee's new consultant's side business with Four Pillars under wraps and suggested Lee do the same. Although Lee didn't respond, under Chinese custom his silence implied his acceptance.

On July 20, 1989, before flying back to Ohio, Lee visited the Four Pillars research facility offices in San Chung City. There Lee met with Kao to hammer out details of his first year of consulting. Kao told him the company was keenly interested in the adhesive rheology area, Lee's specialty. They created a rough-draft plan and Lee received his first year's bounty from the company's finance manager: a check from Four Pillars for $25,000. To hide Lee's connection to Four Pillars the check had been made out to Lee's sister-in-law, who would later wire the funds to him. Lee's mother-in-law had suggested this scheme, without consulting her daughter first, since Lee's sister-in-law lived in the United States and it would be relatively simple to redirect the money to Lee's bank account. Lee would have to cover the 6 percent Taiwanese payroll tax she would be charged. Sometimes Four Pillars paid Lee in traveler's checks. But virtually all the payments he would receive from Four Pillars over the next several years would be laundered through his relatives, "to conceal the illegal conspiracy between Four Pillars and Dr. Lee," prosecutors would allege.

If Lee's silence in response to Yang's offer at dinner hadn't been a clear enough signal, it didn't take long for Lee to get sniffing for glue. Twenty-five thousand dollars was a lot of money and he was nervous about proving his worth—and worthiness. Less than two weeks after accepting his first payment, Lee, now back on the job with Avery, mailed Yang a letter on July 31, 1989. Laying out his strategy for his first year of consulting, he informed Yang that Avery Dennison's Fasson Roll division had a 40 percent to 45 percent share of the label market in the United States "because it has a unique technical service department, which is absolutely an important key link and which is worth our learning." Although he had been with Avery for three years and Four Pillars less than two weeks, Lee chose the word "our" to characterize his relationship to Yang. The moment Victor Lee agreed to work in secret for Four Pillars he began to identify with the company—and the country of his birth. "This is not uncommon in Chinese communities around the world, where ancestral ties are strong, a prime reason China's national intelligence agency targets overseas Chinese as operatives," points out former CIA analyst Guy Dubois.

Victor Lee promised Yang he would supply information, "most" of which would be "taken from Fasson/Avery, so please make sure to treat them as confidential material," adding that he "would do

[his] utmost to collect" data and hereby provide "benefit for Four Pillars." He enclosed an "Outline of Action Plan for the Future," which he based on discussions with Kao at their Taipei meeting. The plan took up topics like application engineering, process and engineering development, product development, rheology, technical services, and test methods.

Department of Justice trial attorney Marc Zwillinger characterizes Lee's "consulting" activities as "a massive technology transfer" from Avery to Four Pillars. "He stood on the shoulders of people who did the work for Avery and gave it to Four Pillars," Zwillinger says. "Avery had an advanced rheology department and Lee was in charge of doing their new formulations, so Four Pillars treated Avery as one big R&D lab."

Lee didn't bother to tell Yang that by agreeing to consult for Four Pillars he was violating a confidentiality agreement he had inked with Avery, which, in part, read:

> During and after his employment with Avery, [Dr. Lee] will not disclose or appropriate any information for his use or for the use of others, except as has been expressly authorized in writing by an officer at Avery. [Dr. Lee] shall not remove any writings containing information from the premises or possession of Avery or its clients unless [Dr. Lee] has obtained express authorization in writing from Avery to do so.

Also, as part of regular corporate protocol, Avery Dennison routinely required all of its employees to sign conflict of interest and legal ethical conduct questionnaires, which Lee did at least half a dozen times over the period he says he moonlighted for his adopted company.

Lee waffles when asked if he ever felt he was doing anything wrong by passing Avery Dennison information to Four Pillars. "I realized that some of the things I did, the company may not like it," Lee said at trial. "In that sense, I was wrong." Lee went on to say that he was responding "to their interaction to me," referring to the Yangs and C. K. Kao, his old teacher. When he dealt with Kao he says he didn't feel he was doing something particularly wrong. "My mind was," he says, "I was helping a friend."

In early August 1989, a few days after submitting his dramatic sounding "Plan of Action," Lee shipped two separate parcels of materials to Four Pillars. In the first he enclosed two rheology reports prepared by Avery senior research scientist Dr. E. P. Chang. The academic papers disclosed details about Avery Dennison's master curves, which are to adhesives what printing plates are to paper money or source code is to software: the keys to figuring out exactly how an adhesive is formulated. This would be the equivalent of an Asian soft drink maker learning the formula for Coca-Cola.

In his note to Yang, Lee characterized the reports as "extremely confidential," and "the fruit of painstaking work of Avery Research Center over a period of years." But Yang could have ascertained this on his own by looking at the "CONFIDENTIAL" stamps placed prominently on the documents. Lee also threw in a "summary of his work in rheology . . . between May 1986 and April 1988," which, since it was performed while he was working for Avery, technically belonged to Avery.

He promised the report would help Four Pillars "catch up" to Avery "within the shortest possible time." The second package contained even more adhesive gold: master curves for Avery's AT-1, an all-temperature emulsion acrylic adhesive, and GP-1, a general-purpose permanent adhesive.

That was just the first shipment. A few days later Lee hustled off details of an emulsion adhesive formulation from Avery Research Center, which he dubbed "a new weapon marketed as recently as September this year," that could not be gleaned through reverse engineering or by any other method. He posted an internal software program he himself had coded, which dealt with "time-temperature superposition" and enabled the automated generation and analysis of master curves.

Lee whiled away hours in Avery's labs, running comparison tests between Four Pillars and Avery Dennison adhesives for computer applications like address labels, and in the process, according to government attorneys, disclosed confidential information about Avery Dennison that "allowed Four Pillars to understand how to improve its products to compete more effectively in the marketplace." He discussed Avery hot-melt adhesive technology, in which Lee was a leading researcher, disclosed Avery Fasson Roll Division's sales for 1989 (property of Avery Dennison), and detailed the properties of paper products used in specific applications—specifications that offered Four Pillars the ability to create copies of Avery Dennison's paper stocks. Hell-bent on proving his value early on, Lee accomplished all of this in the first couple of years.

In the seven years he considered himself part of the Four Pillars family, Lee shipped off a staggering collection of material, ten formulas in all, according to prosecutors, plus five dozen books, research papers containing proprietary information, internal memos, and economic figures. Lee estimates he had between twenty and thirty conversations with Four Pillars employees and sent ten mailings. Some more highlights: three testing methods for silicone, which he himself described as "confidential"; Gillette's self-testing Duracell battery labels; a report by an Avery senior scientist on five-roll silicone coating technology, a science that requires many years of experience to master; and technical reports on modeling, curl control, and moisture measurement, also block-stamped "CONFIDENTIAL." With this data, Department of Justice attorneys assert, Four Pillars was able to lower costs and improve the quality of its paper-based products. Lee, by taking annual trips to Taiwan paid for by Four Pillars, provided material in person, lecturing company employees on technical matters. Also, by his own count, he gave five separate presentations to Four Pillars personnel, in Taiwan, Newark, New Jersey, and Cleveland. Avery Dennison says Lee's annual trips to Taiwan did not raise any suspicions inside the company because Lee was, after all, Taiwanese.

Which Lee worked to his full advantage. At a downtown Taipei apartment, Lee says he slipped Four Pillars key information about "Aquarius"—a specialty-paper project on which Avery says it spent $10 million to develop. When he couldn't nab the goods himself, usually because they were outside his area of expertise, he turned to unwitting accomplices within Avery, who assisted him by passing on reports and sharing passwords. According to Zwillinger, the info thefts were so common Lee even a stashed a collection of preaddressed mailing labels made out to Yang.

The only ebb in the flow of information occurred during the joint venture discussions the companies held starting in early 1993, when Four Pillars' vice president C. K. Kao told Lee to halt his activities for a while. Two years later, Lee says, Yang called him with the news that talks had broken off and a joint venture between the two companies was no longer a possibility. Lee claims Yang told him to continue doing what he had been doing on behalf of Four Pillars.

It would all come tumbling down in the spring of 1996, when Avery received the résumé of a young Four Pillars scientist, Jean (Jong) Guo, from Management Recruiters, a head-hunting firm. After a stint with Four Pillars, following a job with Monsanto in the United States, Guo wanted to return to the States because his son suffered from asthma and Taiwan's poor air quality exacerbated his condition. Guo's résumé was passed around Lee's group at Fasson Roll Division, with everyone receiving a copy. After a slate of interviews, Guo was offered the job (starting salary: $70,000) over the phone by Prem Krish, who followed up with a letter dated May 15, 1996.

Guo had "by a pretty wide margin" outscored "any other candidate that we interviewed," says Avery executive Thomas Allen.

According to the government, Lee contacted Yang to warn him of Guo's hiring, afraid the former Four Pillars scientist would blow his cover. Yang was determined to stop Avery from completing the hire. So on June 7, 1996, Yang penned a letter to the company, complaining about Avery's poaching of one of his key employees, Guo. It violated business ethics and put Four Pillars' proprietary information at risk, he said.

Avery assured Yang its hiring of Guo was not a competitive threat to Four Pillars and promised his activities would be restricted to products that did not directly compete with Four Pillars' products. Yang hustled off a strong response on July 25, 1996, arguing that Guo had had unfettered access to "valuable proprietary information" and would be in breach of his "noncompetition agreement." He threatened to bring the whole weight of his company down on Guo, telling Avery he would sue Guo, which could keep Avery's new prized recruit tied up in litigation for years, and withhold vested severance pay if he jumped from Four Pillars to Avery Dennison.

Yang knew which buttons to push. He was experienced in the art of litigation, having spent years wrestling in Taiwanese courts over patent rights. He had no intention of backing down; neither did Avery. It was Guo who did. He reluctantly informed the Avery manager who had first recruited him, Dr. Krish, that under the circumstances he could not join the company. Instead he moved to Massachusetts to take a job with Solutia Inc., formerly the chemical businesses of Monsanto, a company not in the tape or label business.

But Guo felt bitter toward the man who had denied him the job he coveted. He remained in touch with Krish, and in an August conversation had a surprise for his newfound friend at Avery. Guo told Krish that an Ohio-based Avery Dennison employee, Ten Hong "Victor" Lee, had for seven years been working as a so-called consultant for Four Pillars. His source was unimpeachable: C. K. Kao, the Four Pillars vice president who was in charge of handling Lee. Kao had also let slip that Lee was rewarded with substantial amounts of money and given free round-trip passage to Taiwan once a year. Krish was aghast. He informed Avery, and the detective agency Kroll Associates was hired to check into it. It didn't take long for detectives to dig up enough dirt to justify calling in the FBI.

It took two months for the feds to work up a case against Lee, tapping his phones, checking his calling patterns, and quietly subpoenaing his bank and credit card records. In the end all they had amassed for their trouble were hearsay allegations of industrial espionage coupled with some suspicious activity on Lee's part. They would need more if they were going to hit Lee with accusations of corporate espionage. The FBI agreed a sting operation was in order.

The Bureau worked with Avery executive Allen to put together the sting packet, which they decided would include information that Four Pillars would find irresistible: a faked Asian expansion memo, listing Four Pillars as a potential employee and R&D poaching target, plus details on a recent business venture in India. After Lee took the bait the FBI waited for him to do something with the memo—mail it, fax it, recite the contents over the telephone—but Lee did nothing. After two months the FBI ran out of patience and confronted him.

Lee was called to a meeting of the international studies group by his supervisor on March 6, 1997, except that none of the other members were there. Krish, who walked Lee to the door, promptly did an about-face as soon as Lee entered the room, leaving him to face three men in suits alone.

"Sit down," ordered FBI Special Agent Michael Bartholomew. "We have something to talk to you about." The bearded, balding G-man said there wasn't going to be an international business meeting today.

Lee did as he was told. He didn't know what this was about.

Bartholomew told him he had been caught on camera taking confidential material.

At first Lee got all mealy-mouthed, insisting he was innocent, claiming he had not actually read the stolen plans, that he was just a "technical guy."

But Bartholomew persisted, asking Lee about an alleged improper relationship with Four Pillars. Before long Lee's will to resist crumbled and in Bartholomew's words he began to "gratuitously" confess to a host of sins he had committed on behalf of Four Pillars. This first meeting with Bartholomew lasted about three hours, with Lee offering a detailed oral confession. He was instructed to turn in his corporate credit cards to Avery. The next day Lee gave Bartholomew the first installment of his Four Pillars correspondence, although it would take him two more trips over the course of the week to collect the rest. Lee also agreed to tape-record phone conversations with personnel at Four Pillars for the Bureau.

The company engaged in a vigorous internal debate. Should Avery just fire Lee and get on with the business of making sticky things? Or would the best strategy be to drag Four Pillars through both the criminal and civil courts? That would mean going public with the embarrassing admission that a competitor had been able to steal valuable Avery R&D for seven years. How would its stockholders react? Would the business press rally around Avery, or would the company be portrayed as a laughingstock that couldn't keep a secret? "It's easy to sort of sweep things under the rug," says Robenalt. "But there was a debate. They thought it through."

The company decided to pulverize Four Pillars.

Over the next month Lee, in a dozen meetings with Bartholomew, prepared a detailed confession for use by Avery in its civil suit and the government in its criminal investigations against Four Pillars. Showing no mercy, Avery gleefully turned the screws on the disgraced scientist. Dominic Surprenant, the company's outside counsel, informed Lee that his liability would be "almost certain to run into the millions of dollars, and, as an absolute minimum, in excess of $600,000." Surprenant also noted that "the most modest recovery . . . would wipe . . . [Lee] out." That was, unless both Lee and his wife, who admitted she knew of her husband's activities, signed an agreement the company was drafting, one that would ensure Lee's complete cooperation.

The government wanted him to sign a separate deal, a plea that would get Lee to flip to its side. Although Lee was in a tight spot he did have some leverage. Both the government and Avery needed him to provide and interpret the hard evidence that would allow them to emerge victorious. Not only was Lee an exacting scientist, he had been a meticulous record keeper, having taken his sideline consulting business seriously. Lee had stowed copies and files of most of his correspondence with Four Pillars over the years, which he used to track expenses. His usual practice was to make three copies of every piece of correspondence, sending the original to Yang cc-ing C. K. Kao and Sally Yang, and keeping a copy for himself.

But his obligations wouldn't end with just turning over records. Lee would also have to actively participate in a sting operation against Four Pillars. It would begin with Lee convincing Yang to come to the United States, since the short arm of American federal law didn't extend into Taiwan, then, on camera, inducing him to accept planted material. If Lee played his part right he would get off light with no prison time and owing Avery Dennison $160,000—the amount Four Pillars had given him. It would devastate him financially but was better than being in the hole for millions to Avery.

Making the best of a bad situation wasn't doing much for Lee's emotional state. He was feeling isolated and afraid, his reputation in tatters. He had maintained a friendship with P. Y. and Sally Yang, who had stayed with him and his family at his Mentor, Ohio, home. He had grown especially fond of Sally, who would call him for advice on technical problems Four Pillars was having, or for tutoring in her science studies, freely tapping his expertise in rheology and high-speed release. In one phone call she told him she loved America, "the best country in the world," and told Lee she planned to soon leave Four Pillars. Lee knew it wasn't fair she should get caught up in all of this.

As Lee further spiraled into a funk over what he called "his situation," Avery attorneys presented him with a document they had drafted. In it, Avery had codified a number of promises it wished to extract. He promised to fork over the agreed sum to Avery and to cooperate fully in the company's investigations, which included granting consent to name Lee as a party defendant in any action, meeting with Avery Dennison lawyers upon demand, and giving testimony in both the civil and criminal proceedings.

It didn't take long for the pressure to further erode his judgment. Torn by the tenuousness of his own situation, the cutting impact it was having on his family, and the guilt he was suffering for betraying the Yangs, Lee began to act irrationally. Clearly conflicted, depending on his mood he ranged from being helpful and solicitous with government agents to taciturn and withholding.

"He was a very difficult witness to work with," says Zwillinger. "Lee betrayed everyone. He betrayed Avery, which had made him sign a disclosure agreement; he betrayed his coconspirators by cooperating with the government, and he betrayed the government when he lied."

This would come back to haunt Lee, affecting his deals with prosecutors and his former employer. Before turning over his files and documentation to the FBI, Lee took a stab at shielding Yang and in one swoop violated the agreements he had put his name to. He secreted away the final two pages of a six-page letter he had sent to Yang in 1993, and deleted a particularly damning sentence in another: "Buying books is easy," he had written, but "getting secret or confidential documents is harder." By tampering with the evidence, Lee committed what is known in defense-attorney-speak as "a felony stupid," a misdemeanor that turns ugly when the perpetrator does something to worsen the situation, usually resulting in a felony rap.

At the same time, Lee continued to offer explicit details of his conduct with Four Pillars over the previous seven years until Department of Justice attorneys were confident they had enough to launch phase two of the investigation: a sting to capture P. Y. Yang on American soil.

The problem was this could take time to put together. The usual strategy would be to let the scheme unfold naturally, but Avery was in a hurry to seek vengeance. "We were telling them we were only willing to wait so long before we'd take more serious actions," Allen admitted in a deposition. "If you guys [at the FBI] aren't going to make this happen for another six or eight months, we're going to consider not following your advice and doing something else on our own. I think that kind of prompted them to try to arrange a meeting that would happen sooner rather than later."

On August 3, 1997, after agents had briefed him on what to say and how to say it, Lee telephoned Yang in Taiwan to find out when the Four Pillars founder would be visiting the United States.

As agents eavesdropped, Lee, seeking to boost Yang's incentive to make the trip, told him he would be able to get detailed information about new emulsion adhesive technology, but that would have to be discussed in person. According to prosecutors Yang also expressed interest in Avery's Far East business plans.

With the government's carefully orchestrated sting, complete with manufactured trade secrets, and Lee's time-tested relationship with the Yangs, the operation went down without a hitch and preparation for trial proceedings began.

Avery–Four Pillars wasn't the first Economic Espionage Act case involving Taiwanese. The Yangs even referred to it in the hours before they were incarcerated: the Taxol case, when three Taiwanese—Kai-Lo Hsu, Chester S. Ho, and Jessica Chou working on behalf of Yuen Foong Paper Company—were accused of violating America's economic espionage laws. It was the first case charged under the act (the second involved an employee of Gillette trying to walk off with the plans to the company's Mach-3 razor; Avery Dennison was the third), and it was coming to a head as the Four Pillars–Avery case crept forward. In the Taxol case the defendants were in jail for seeking to obtain the formulas, methods, and processes for producing the anticancer drug Taxol, created by Bristol-Myers Squibb.

The conspiracy kicked off in the summer of 1995, when Chou, manager of business development for the Yuen Foong Paper Company, asked a technology information broker about Taxol. Chou contacted the tech broker repeatedly over the next six months to learn about Taxol manufacturing techniques and distribution. Yuen Foong was interested in a pharmaceutical product because it wanted to diversify into biotechnology, and the easiest way to do this was to steal it from more technologically advanced nations. When the info broker said Bristol-Myers would not be inclined to share secrets, Kai-Lo Hsu, technical director for Yuen Foong's operations, allegedly retorted, "We'll get [it] another way," and ordered him to pay off Bristol-Myers employees. It took more than a year for Hsu and Chou to work out the nitty-gritty and negotiate a price. The tech broker then informed them he had lined up a Bristol-Myers scientist willing to trade information about Taxol for money and scheduled a meeting at the Four Seasons Hotel in Philadelphia for June 1997.

It was a setup. The "corrupt" scientist was an employee of Bristol-Myers working closely with John Hartmann, an undercover FBI agent posing as an information broker specializing in technology. During the meeting, attended by Hsu, Chester Ho, a professor of biotechnology and director of the Biotechnology Innovation Center, and another unidentified scientist, the man from Bristol-Myers talked at length about the history and background of Taxol, sharing papers that outlined specific processes and data relating to Taxol's manufacture. All of the documents were labeled with Bristol-Myers's identification and were block-stamped "CONFIDENTIAL."

Hsu, Ho, and the other Yuen Foong employee read the documents and had the Bristol-Myers scientist field "numerous" queries relating to Taxol technology. After Hartmann and the Bristol-Myers scientist left the room, the FBI broke in and arrested Hsu and Ho, who were charged with six counts of wire fraud and two counts of criminal activity under the Economic Espionage Act of 1996, which included attempted theft of trade secrets and conspiracy to steal trade secrets.

After the indictment was handed down, the defense requested in discovery copies of the Bristol-Myers documents containing the information about Taxol that had been leaked to Hsu and Ho. For their clients to be guilty of stealing trade secrets, the defense attorneys reasoned, the material disclosed to them would also have to be considered trade secrets.

"To prove trade secrecy theft, you first have to prove there is a trade secret," says Chicago attorney Marc Halligan, author of *Trade Secrets Case Digest*. If the defense could show that the information in the Bristol-Myers papers was not really a trade secret, or that it could have been obtained elsewhere, or that the company had been lax in documenting the steps it took in protecting its proprietary information, it was possible the judge would throw the case out.

Zwillinger, who also worked on the Bristol-Myers case, realized the Economic Espionage Act of 1996 would be gutted if he were to willy-nilly hand over the victim's trade secrets to the defense. No company would ever come forward again. Department of Justice lawyers believed Bristol-Myers had acted courageously and the last thing they needed was to burn the first corporation that brought them a case. The government filed a motion for a protective order to prevent the disclosure of the alleged trade secrets contained in the Bristol-Myers documents. When it lost it looked like the law that Congress had passed was destined to be banished to the Book of Irrelevance.

But the act was saved on appeal with a motion penned by Zwillinger. The Third Circuit agreed with him that the government didn't have to prove that an actual trade secret was used in an investigation of an economic espionage crime; the government could satisfy its burden by proving beyond a reasonable doubt that the defendant believed the material constituted a trade secret; whether it was or was not a trade secret was irrelevant.

The Third Circuit also ruled that the defendants didn't require the Taxol documents in its defense against charges of conspiracy. "Moreover," Halligan points out in his *Digest,* "it further encourages enforcement actions by protecting owners who might otherwise be reluctant to cooperate in prosecutions for fear of further exposing their trade secrets to public view, thus further devaluing or even destroying their worth." The Third Circuit concluded it was highly unlikely that Congress would have wanted the courts to risk the security of trade secrets in pursuing their prosecution.

This ruling would have a sharp impact on the Avery–Four Pillars case. To lure Yang to Cleveland, the FBI had used a soon-to-expire patent owned by Avery and a faked Asian expansion plan as bait. Clearly neither qualified as a trade secret. But that didn't mean Yang couldn't be tried for attempted trade secrecy theft under the law.

To complicate the charges, the other trade secrecy breaches, the formulas that Lee had allegedly passed on to Four Pillars, had occurred before the Economic Espionage Act of 1996 had become law. Which is why government attorneys ended up charging the Yangs with nineteen various counts of mail and wire fraud, in addition to the two counts of breaking the nation's anti–economic espionage laws. (Those covered the hotel room sting.) In the malaise that is the U.S. criminal court system, mail and wire fraud are the kinds of charges prosecutors levy when they can't get a defendant on anything else. But the Taxol ruling made it easier on the prosecution. Now the material that had set the whole conspiracy in motion couldn't effectively be assailed in court.

Marc Zwillinger knew whatever new case law the Taxol case spawned would have an immediate impact on his prosecution of Four Pillars. Days after Peter Toren had been assigned the case in Ohio, Zwillinger, then a new hiree, had been brought on board from Washington, D.C., to assist. A few months in, Toren decided he didn't have the time or manpower to pursue the case and passed it off to Zwillinger. It was the young attorney's first Department of Justice case, but one he fully expected to plea bargain like the other EEA cases.

Fresh out of law school, the then-twenty-eight-year-old was learning on the fly. But Zwillinger, a self-professed electronic-gadget freak who often puts in eighty-hour weeks, was no typical rookie. With classic regular-guy good looks and a Dockers-Gap-chinos outlook on life, Zwillinger had always been an overachiever, possessing a keen aptitude for the law and technology. His parents, previously divorced stockbrokers with children older than he, had raised him as an only child in the glossy suburb of Scarsdale, a forty-five-minute rail commute from Manhattan. Zwillinger jokes he was nine years old when he first realized he wanted to be a lawyer, after he played Snow White's defense attorney in his fourth-grade class play, "The Trial of Snow White."

After maintaining an A- average at Tufts and achieving a perfect score on his law boards, he was accepted at Harvard Law School in 1991. For the three years he was in school he volunteered with Harvard Defenders, providing free legal assistance to people in need. He also interned with the Senate Judiciary Committee when Senator Joseph Biden was chairman; the hot issue of the day: flag-burning. After graduation he worked as a litigator at Kirkland & Ellis, a Chicago law firm, before jumping to the Department of Justice. "I have always been interested in the point where law and politics meet," Zwillinger says. "I didn't take a traditional path to being a prosecutor." Three weeks after Toren had okayed Department of Justice involvement with the Avery Dennison case Zwillinger was brought up to speed. It became immediately apparent that one of the most problematic areas would be the relationship between the government and Avery, a relationship that Zwillinger, when pressed, would describe as "difficult."

Avery announced its intention to press forward with its $100 million civil action against Four Pillars—a move that would gravely interfere with the EEA case—and in a high-handed manner acted like it was doing the government a favor in even bothering to assist with the criminal case. "From Avery Dennison's position it was: A crime had been reported and when they asked us to help out, we helped out," says Robenot simply.

Although Zwillinger says that in the end the adhesives maker was "a good corporate citizen," the government and Avery did "bump heads over their civil case. We needed their help and they were pursuing their own case," he says.

Zwillinger knew if he couldn't convince Avery to postpone its civil case until after the criminal trial, he could still get what he wanted by outmaneuvering its lawyers. "As a prosecutor you are not a bill collector," he says. " You don't take on a case if there is a civil trial. It's one or the other. " As 1997 drew to a close and Avery plunged ahead with its decision to pursue its civil action against Four Pillars, Zwillinger struck.

There was no way he was going to be a footstool for some legal jackal from corporate America. Zwillinger moved to immediately stay the civil case and received support from a surprise corner, the defense. Yang's lawyers joined the government in moving to postpone, which made for strange bedfellows.

"You had DOJ and the defendants on one side and Avery Dennison, the victim, on the other," explains Zwillinger. He successfully moved to stay Victor Lee's civil testimony. Lee's deposition had not yet been taken in the civil investigation and without it neither Avery Dennison nor the defendants could proceed with their investigations. As a result, nobody wanted to go ahead with the civil case. Depositions would have to wait until after the criminal matter was decided.

Zwillinger had temporarily reined in the victim, a victim that unfortunately refused to act like one. He had a signed confession from one of the coconspirators. He had the two defendants on film cutting away "CONFIDENTIAL" markings off a known competitor's documents. And because of a motion he himself had written and filed in the Taxol matter, the law was also clearly on his side.

He thought he had a slam dunk of a case. But when Zwillinger met Yang's new attorneys, he realized he was in for the fight of his young legal life.

4

The Kite

As a mole, Victor Lee put Avery in a sticky situation. But he was strictly an amateur, tapped for his access to information. How would a trained spy approach collecting on a multinational corporation? And what would he do if he had a tight deadline?

That was the dilemma facing SCIP board member William De-Genaro. He had been awarded a lucrative assignment from Schwan's Sales Enterprises Inc., a food company based in Marshall, Minnesota, to find out about a new product that promised to revolutionize frozen pizza. The target was Kraft, the largest packaged food company in the country, which had perfected a new type of "rising crust" pizza it had been test-marketing under the name Di-Giorno. It was the winter of 1997 and up to then it was often hard to taste the difference between a frozen pizza and the cardboard box it was packaged in.

Schwan's, which marketed store-bought pizza under the brand name Tony's, had heard that Kraft, a subsidiary of cigarette maker Philip Morris Companies, was planning a massive advertising campaign designed to position DiGiorno's as the only frozen pizza to taste like fresh, out-of-the-oven, pizza-parlor pizza. In preparation,

Schwan's was gearing up for a major food fight. But if it were to have any chance, it would have to know how fast and furious Kraft, which already sold frozen pizza under the brands Tombstone and Jack's, planned to roll out DiGiorno nationwide. This way it could create a counterstrategy. To do this, however, the company had to know the exact location and production capacity of a plant it knew Kraft had constructed in Sussex, Wisconsin—what type of equipment the plant housed, the number of production lines, what types and sizes of pizzas were being produced there, and, most important, how many pies were coming off the assembly line each day.

DeGenaro's problem was that Schwan's needed the information fast, and it would be nearly impossible for him to get it without resorting to subterfuge. As a board member of the Society of Competitive Intelligence Professionals, he knew SCIP's rules governing collection activities are clear: You can't dupe an unsuspecting employee into giving you what you want, nor can you misrepresent who you are. But Kraft wouldn't just hand over the information to a competitor it was intent on running out of the market. So DeGenaro did what many of his SCIP colleagues espousing open-source collection do. He subcontracted the work to someone else, a "kite" or "go-to guy," who, in addition to being able to get the information the job required, would provide DeGenaro a valuable service: plausible deniability. DeGenaro could fly the kite out there and let him do whatever needed doing to get the information, but if a storm surfaced in the form of a lawsuit or charges of corporate espionage, he could claim he had no idea what his subcontractor was doing. This was, of course, disingenuous.

DeGenaro had carefully cultivated the image of a man of the world; celebrated by his peers for his ability to keep a rapt audience up until dawn with sordid tales of corporate intrigue. Half the SCIP community thought DeGenaro was former CIA; the other half was convinced he was former NSA. The truth is he came out of the Department of Defense. He had headed the competitive intelligence department at 3M, then went on to start his own firm out of Sarasota, Florida, and a school called the Centre for Operational Business Intelligence, which he ran with John Nolan, another SCIP scion. With Schwan's eagerly awaiting the information, DeGenaro phoned Marc Barry, founder of the corporate intelligence firm C³I Analytics of New York, who had gotten the job done for DeGenaro half a dozen times in the past.

Barry, an Irish streetwise redhead in his early thirties, had made a name for himself as an expert "humint" (human intelligence) man working undercover to infiltrate Asian organized crime networks that controlled the distribution of counterfeit goods in the United States, as well as tracking phony pharmaceuticals, foodstuffs, and airplane parts. Some of his clients included Borden, Guess? Jeans, Nike, Warner Bros., and Bausch & Lomb. He can spot a Kate Spade knockoff from across the street and had taken part in dozens of raids to bust up counterfeiting rings. Born in Dorchester, "the murder capital of Boston," Barry single-handedly drafted anticounterfeiting laws passed unanimously by the legislatures in three states—Georgia, Rhode Island, and Texas—giving the police the right to seize the personal bank accounts and other assets of individuals caught manufacturing counterfeit goods. Under his statutes seized revenues were then plowed into local law enforcement coffers. Cops, already stretched thin, had been notoriously lax in coming down on product counterfeiters. Giving them a profit motive, however, spurred them to action.

Ironically, the major opposition to the legislation came from the lawyers who represent the companies whose products are being illegally copied. If Barry's law was adopted it meant there would be nothing left to sue over. So when an industry trade organization run primarily by $400-an-hour attorneys, the International Anti-Counterfeiting Coalition, Inc. (IACC), tried to undermine him in the state legislatures, Barry swiped the organization's trademark when it forgot to reregister it.

He eventually gave it back with a smirk.

As a private investigator who had used more than his share of clever ruses to glean tightly held information, he finds the SCIP ethical guidelines involving disclosure hypocritical. "In my mind I am being hired to acquire sensitive information that my client cannot otherwise get himself," he says. "I have enormous multinational clients and in some instances I work for both the legal and the strategic marketing departments within the same company. The irony of the situation is that while deception, trickery, and a clever ruse will make you the subject of water-cooler folklore in the legal department, that same behavior might get you fired in the strategic marketing department if they expect you to abide by SCIP ethical rules."

This time, the corporation would be Schwan's, which earned an extra-thick slice of its $3 billion from frozen pizza sales. The company realized that if Kraft had found a solution to the problem with packaged pizza, which required it to be precooked, resulting in a gummy, flavorless crust, this meant there loomed a monstrous opportunity.

Like many things that have become a recognizable (and profitable) piece of Americana, pizza made its way to New York City in the latter half of the nineteenth century with an influx of immigrants. Although it is most certainly an Italian invention, many of the ingredients, ironically, also emigrated from elsewhere. Tomatoes, at first an ornamental plant thought to be poisonous, made their way to Italy via Mexico and Peru; the Greeks, who ate a type of flat, round bread they called *plankuntos,* originated the idea of using bread as a plate; mozzarella, created from the milk of the water buffalo, can be traced to seventh-century India. In 1905, an Italian immigrant, Gennaro Lombardi, opened the nation's first pizzeria (Lombardi's) in New York, but it wasn't until the 1950s that pizza went mass-market with the establishment of national chains like Pizza Hut and Shakey's.

Nowadays, Americans consume the equivalent of 100 acres of pizza a day at pizzerias and at home—the most popular topping: pepperoni, which sits on about a third of all slices—with the average American family spending almost $350 a year on frozen pizza alone. Although sales of store-bought pies equal about $2 billion annually, pizza parlors nationwide earn fifteen times that. Since much of the dough used in the crusts consumed at pizza joints is frozen anyway, a packaged product that cooked up fresh in the oven could tap into this $30 billion market.

Schwan's already knew the secret behind DiGiorno: pumping yeast into the raw crust, a formula Kraft had gotten in 1992 when it bought Jack's, a modest Wisconsin-based frozen pizza maker. At the time, analysts said it was a shrewd move to complement Kraft's pricier Tombstone brand. Little did they know that Kraft was also gaining some fancy R&D with its paltry $5 million purchase. The first to get a better-tasting pizza into grocery stores would have an enviable advantage. Schwan's had to know how far behind Kraft it was with its own rising-dough pizza. That's why it hired DeGenaro, and that's why he, unbeknownst to Schwan's, turned to his go-to guy, Marc Barry.

After accepting the job through a DeGenaro associate named Ray Pucci, who Barry says "pays short but promptly," he bought a $10 prepaid phone card from a nearby grocery so his calls couldn't be traced. He set up a bogus voice mail and fax-forwarding line with a company called American Voice Mail. Both accounts were created under the 414 area code, which covers Sussex, Wisconsin. This way, Barry could collect his messages and faxes from his office in New York, yet his targets would be under the impression he was local. Then he put on a pot of espresso, lit up a cigarette, and after running some routine Internet searches, grabbed the only tool he would need: the telephone.

Pucci had already told him where the factory was located. Barry figured someone in the town government would know details about it. "Politicians are easily manipulated because they are usually eager to take credit for things. Getting a local hack from some town economic development committee to spill on Kraft by baiting him with a bullshit line about how wonderful the new jobs would be for the local economy would be a piece of cake," Barry says. He phoned the chamber of commerce and posed as a reporter from the *Wall Street Journal.* It took him exactly one minute to get the address of the Tombstone pizza plant, located on Susan Road. Barry took a swig of caffeine and dialed the Sussex town assessor's office, where he learned from an employee that Kraft was being assessed taxes for a new 143,914-square-foot plant, no questions asked.

Barry knew that, America being America, Kraft wouldn't be able to begin construction of its plant without permits, so he created a mythical persona, an environmentalist he called Curtis Walton, a name he plucked out of the air. He wrote it down because often at the end of a phone conversation a person will ask, "What was your name again?" and he didn't want to forget. (It had happened before.) Barry dialed the fire department and town building inspectors, since both usually have blueprints for local manufacturing plants. He claimed he was calling on behalf of an environmental advocacy nonprofit organization called EcoNet and was researching an article for the *EcoNews* about excessive fluoro-hydrocarbons being emitted from the Sussex plant. The fire department didn't bite and the building inspectors weren't in. After several calls, Barry managed to get someone at the building inspector's office on the line, who told him there was nothing she could do until her boss returned.

"But I'm on deadline," Barry-cum-Walton said. "Isn't there anything you can do?"

"My boss is so much better at reading these plans than I am," she said. "I'm afraid I'd miss something."

"Any help you could give would be greatly appreciated."

"I don't know—"

Eventually Barry wore her down with his pleading and she took pity. As she read off the contents of the plans, even though he was recording the conversation, Barry scrawled notes just in case the tape broke or there was a glitch. Often you only get one shot and he wanted to make sure he got it all.

"This was not a new plant, but rather additions are being added onto an existing plant," the woman informed him. This made sense. To keep transportation costs down Kraft would want to keep its pizza production in a centralized location and close to key ingredients. "The 143,914-square-foot addition was designed by Stahlman Engineering of New London, New Hampshire—"

"Stahlman? How do you spell that?" Barry asked.

"S-t-a-h-l-m-a-n."

"Of New London, New Hampshire?"

"Yes. And built by Maas Brothers—M-a-a-s—Construction of Watertown, Wisconsin."

She recited the details the expansion permit covered: additional warehousing, more bakery space, a new recycling building. When she got into the nitty-gritty of what equipment was going to be housed in the new facility, Barry peppered her with questions and began to draw a map.

". . . three compressor rooms," she said, "a ten-below-zero freezer and high-rise freezers—"

"How many?"

"Two. A label paste room, meat cooler, and cheese coolers, a chemical storage room, something called a vestibule conveyor belt system, bakery waterfall oiler, several sauce and topping lines–"

"How many sauce and topping lines?"

"It doesn't say."

"Okay, go on."

"A Grotter PepperMatic, four spiral freezers–"

"How far from the conveyor belt are the freezers?"

"Around the corner, about eight feet away. A wheat dock, a loading dock–"

"How big is the loading dock?"

"Um, 1,906 square feet."

"Where is it?"

"It's been relocated between the bakery and the recycling room."

Delighted by his score, Barry thanked her and hung up. Four spiral and two high-rise freezers? A 2,000-square-foot loading dock? A bakery waterfall oiler? Although Barry didn't know anything about pizza production, Schwan's certainly did and would be able to make good use of this information. But Barry was far from done. Now came the tricky part: How would he be able to measure the plant's operating capacity? He puffed on a Macanudo miniature cigar and mulled over a strategy. What, he wondered, do all frozen pizzas require? Labels. How would he track labels, though? Besides, there were at least three different styles. Pepperoni, mushrooms? But the plant must use a lot of different toppings. Cheese? No way. Too complicated. Kraft used tons of it, and didn't it manufacture a four-cheese pie? Besides, cheese could be stored for a while, so it wouldn't be much use in trying to figure out how many pizzas come off those conveyor belts. Wheat? Yeast? Oil? Nah, that wouldn't do it. The cardboard boxes? Maybe, except that Tombstone pizzas were packaged in shrink-wrapped plastic, not in a box. About halfway through his cigar, it came to him. Diskettes. Every pizza, whether it came in a box or in shrink-wrapped plastic, sat on a round cardboard diskette. This was the one constant.

Barry picked up the receiver and dialed the Sussex plant. He asked for accounts payable and after the inevitable phone system lag got a voice mail. Immediately he punched zero and when an operator picked up he requested accounts receivable. After another voice mail he ordered the operator to hook him up with another department where a young woman picked up.

"Hi, this is Bobby Royce," Barry said, looking at the name he had just scrawled in his notebook, alongside a fictitious company. "I'm president of Presidential Corrugated Box."

"What can I do for you, Mr. Royce?" the woman asked cheerfully.

Good, Barry thought. "Well, you see, I own a cardboard manufacturing plant, nothing too big, mind you. A local family business. And I figured since I was a local business and you're a local business, well, maybe we could do business together."

"I dunno, sir," she said. "We use an awful lot of cardboard."

"Hmm, I see. What do you think you'd need. Ten, twenty thousand units a month?"

"Oh, no, we'd need more than that."

"How much more?"

"A lot more. We go through hundreds of thousands of units a day. We use Weyerhaeuser. They're the largest."

Barry tried his best to sound disappointed. "Weyerhaeuser, huh. That's way too much output for our plant. But in case you get any spillover and need more, I'll send over some literature."

He got off the phone and logged on to the Internet, where he plugged Weyerhaeuser into Yahoo's search engine to locate its corporate web site. One call to Weyerhaeuser's corporate headquarters and he was given the number of the White Bear Lake facility in Minneapolis, Minnesota, the plant that serviced Wisconsin. He posed as an employee of the purchasing department of Kraft's Tombstone pizza plant who had just taken over the account and claimed there was a discrepancy on some paperwork. He asked how many boxes and disks Weyerhaeuser had shipped to the plant in the last month. But the number the accounts payable department gave him, in the low hundreds of thousands, was much too low compared to what the woman from accounts payable had told him. It didn't make sense. Barry started another cigar and dialed the Kraft Tombstone loading dock.

After a few rings someone picked up and Barry could hear heavy machinery grinding in the background. Reprising his role as Bobby Royce, owner of Presidential Corrugated Box, Barry and the Tombstone worker fell into small talk. Barry figured the guy must be a Green Bay Packers fan, so he pretended the Minnesota Vikings, whom the Packers were scheduled to play that week, were his favorite team. The conversation shifted from Packers legend Vince Lombardi to the right kind of thermos for Wisconsin winters to who manufactures the best work boot. Barry, who had worked as an undercover agent on dozens of loading docks for cargo theft investigations, said he liked Timberlands, but his new friend wore Wolverines. Finally, after building a rapport, Barry started asking questions about cardboard.

"How many pounds of boxes are being moved off that dock for Kraft?" he asked.

The loading dock worker gave him a number even lower than the one Weyerhaeuser had supplied. Now he was really confused. "They come in only once or twice a week," the guy added, trying to be helpful.

"What do you mean?" Barry asked.

"We recycle the boxes."

"I don't get it. You sell your pizzas in the box, right?"

"These are different boxes. These ones get used four times each. We use them to ship the crusts up from Little Chute."

"What the hell is Little Chute?"

"Our crust manufacturing plant. But we're not going to be using cardboard for this much longer. We're moving to plastic for inter-plant shipping, which doesn't have to be recycled." He told Barry the Little Chute factory manufactured most of the crusts, although some came from the Sussex plant. Since September 1997, Kraft had been producing a total of 300,000 pizzas per day, which included the twelve-inch Jack's pizza, as well as eight- and twelve-inch Di-Giorno pizzas. Little Chute was the only plant to make the eight-inch DiGiorno.

Barry thanked the man, then phoned various departments at the Little Chute facility, where he confirmed that the Sussex plant was operating at a capacity of 300,000 pizzas per day, and that it had re-cently begun to make small quantities of rising crust dough as well. He dialed the Sussex plant's production lines manager and claimed he was writing a research paper on food production. "I know you are cranking out 300,000 pizzas a day," he said. "How many pro-duction lines is that?" Five, he was told, but only three run at any one time. Barry then called the building inspector's office and got the lowdown on the Little Chute plant, drafting another detailed map for his client. For good measure he found out that Kraft was also selling stuffed-crust pizza, but not making the crusts. Instead, it had contracted out the work to Nations Pizza in Chicago, Illi-nois, which told him that Kraft was test-marketing pizzas whose crusts were stuffed with cheese and/or pepperoni for Tombstone, and that it was not an exclusive contract so it could supply anyone it wanted.

The total amount of time Barry worked on this caper: a day and a half, most of it waiting for people to call back. But the informa-tion was worth millions to his client. Although DiGiorno was the first of the rising-crust pizzas, a year later Schwan's introduced its own contender under the name Freschetta. Rising-crust pizzas became the fastest-growing food category, with an almost 50 percent increase in sales within a year. DiGiorno quickly rose to become the number one–selling pizza in the nation, but Freschetta, number six, has closed the gap with a 66 percent jump in 1998 sales to $108 million, more than double the rate of DiGiorno. Which is the better tasting pizza? Food reviewers are on record as being enthusiastic about both, but oddly enough, it's been DiGiorno trucks that have been hijacked three separate times by pizza-loving thieves. After one of the heists, when 348 pizzas were stolen, Mike Young, key account manager for Kraft Pizza Co., was quoted as saying, "That was one big party, I guess." And St. Louis County police said they didn't think the theft had anything to do with a massive beer spill that occurred days earlier, when an Anheuser-Busch beer truck turned over.

Barry says he had nothing to do with it.

5

Trade Show Cowboy

"I always feel bad about myself after trade shows—deceiving people, establishing relationships under false pretenses," says Karim Fadel, manager of competitor analysis for PictureTel, a $300 million videoconferencing equipment maker headquartered in Andover, Massachusetts. "But you gotta do what you gotta do. I mean, God will forgive me. I haven't murdered anyone; there are much bigger sins. And I don't think I'll burn in hell because I impersonated a consultant."

Karim Fadel is a corporate spook with a guilty conscience. Not your typical spy material, he believes his most prominent feature, besides his build ("I'm very skinny") and hair ("balding fast"), is an exceedingly large nose. But looks are deceiving, and this works to his benefit. Whereas Jan Herring created his business intelligence unit within Motorola to be above reproach for fear that if he didn't he might end up on the six o'clock news, Fadel admits to using whatever means are necessary to get the skinny on a rival, leaving ethical collecting to those who can afford to lose.

One target-rich stalking ground for competitor intelligence is trade shows, where PictureTel rivals are sitting ducks penned up in standard convention-issue cubicles. He claims everyone in his industry does what he does, although perhaps not to the extreme he takes it. Has he ever been caught? "My bosses don't even know I do this," Fadel says. "Of course, they must know something is up when I get them confidential price lists and distribute them within the company. But they never ask questions, and I'm sure not going to tell them."

As PictureTel likes to say, it lets pictures tell the story of its products and services. Many of them, depending on a customer's needs, go for six figures or more, including intricate hardware that enables users in far-flung locations to simultaneously talk and view one another over a computer network. A hundred salespeople across the globe can meet and discuss strategies without leaving their offices; engineers can collaborate on design specifications and keep tabs on projects, from the blueprint stage to final product demonstrations; a hands-on CEO can address a select group of employees or the whole company all at once, ensuring clear top-down communication and a minimum of budget- and time-sapping miscommunications. A Global 1000 company can hold a corporate town meeting without paying a dime in travel expenses, or videocast its shareholder meetings (which often increases attendance), or transmit pictorially rich press releases hyped up with 3-D graphics and animation, helping a new product to make a splash. If someone misses a broadcast, no problem: He can always view it later at his leisure, since sessions can be archived and viewed at the push of a button.

As with computer hardware and chips, the $8 billion videoconferencing industry, expected to grow to more than $13 billion by 2003, experiences warp-speed change, with technology often out of date as soon as a new product hits the market. The mission of videoconferencing is to make a video call as simple as a telephone call. But this is easier said than done, as there are a number of technological obstacles that make it a brutal business, rife with spying, dirty tricks, and employee poaching. "Nondisclosure agreements, material stamped CONFIDENTIAL, all this means nothing," Fadel says. "We know what our competitors are doing and they know what we are doing."

How do they do this? In Fadel's case, he keeps in touch with dozens of ex-PictureTel employees who have moved over to the competition, namely the two other big players in the market, traditional rival VTEL, based in Austin, Texas, and Polycom, a relative newcomer hailing from San Jose, California, which owes its existence to former key VTEL personnel jumping ship. There are more than a hundred other companies with a chunk of the market—including international megaconcerns like Digital Microwave Corp., Lucent, Siemens, Aethra Telecomunicazioni of Italy, and Korean powerhouses Daewoo Telecom and Samsung, computer industry spitfires Intel and Microsoft, "push" start-ups such as BackWeb that dabble in cybercasting, and web amazon Broadcast.com. But PictureTel, Polycom, and VTEL, all of which focus exclusively on videoconferencing, are ranked the industry's big three.

And what does Fadel consider to be the mother lode of intelligence? Pricing, the key to strategizing against rivals but hard to get. "Pricing is important information to have," Fadel says, "because you have a benchmark to measure yourself with against your competitors. To compete, we have to know our competitors' prices, so we know where their bids are coming in at." And the best source for competitors' pricing information: the competitors themselves, who can usually be found at industry events, with company representatives only too eager to serve.

Trade shows like Las Vegas Comdex, Internet World, CeBIT (the Hannover, Germany, tech wonder of the world), Streaming Media West and TeleCon (both held in California), and Multimedia Com (which changes locales every year) are much more than feel-good events for companies touting new products. They are, in themselves, a multibillion-dollar industry. There are more than 800 trade shows held every year, with companies spending in excess of $10 billion to attend. Many haunt dozens of them every year: Hewlett-Packard set up shop at ninety-four trade shows in 1999; IBM and Siemens, eighty-eight; and Motorola, sixty-five, each anteing up about $1 million just for the exhibit space, then writing it off as a marketing expense. The bigger shows, the Comdexes, CeBits, and Internet Worlds, attract thousands of companies and people from more than 100 countries.

A spy could easily get lost in the hubbub, a fact not lost on PC maker Compaq, which decided to stop attending shows in the early 1990s, convinced it was just helping its rivals collect intelligence; but the chance to tout its products was too tempting, and by century's end Compaq was spending more than $1.3 million annually just on exhibit space.

The convention halls can be cavernous, with row after row of booths usually laid out in grids, each booth housing a company trying to outdo its competitors. CeBIT attracts three-quarters of a million people flowing through the festivities, with live entertainment thrown into the mix of press conferences, announcements, and the ambience of hundreds of thousands of shoes shuffling through the conference hall. To the attendees, it can seem as if neon and fluorescence are in far greater abundance than oxygen. It's hard not to get caught up in the atmosphere, which is why Fadel has developed a whole system for gleaning intelligence from PictureTel rivals: He treats trade show collection like he's "precision bombing," walking in the door and making a beeline for his targets. He usually attends trade shows as a consultant or potential buyer. He says he knows others in his business who wear disguises such as wigs and colored contact lenses, but Fadel prefers to play it straight. Not as straight as some, however. Herring, for example, has also used trade shows to garner information from Motorola foes, but says he gave strict orders to anyone working for him not to misstate their company affiliation. Of course, this didn't stop him from hiring university professors to traipse into convention halls and strike up highly technical conversations with company salespeople to glean the tech specs to new products—and it's not like they wore badges with Motorola printed on them.

There are even schools that teach enrollees how to gather intelligence at a trade show. The Centre for Operational Business Intelligence, run by SCIP members Bill DeGenaro and John Nolan, offers courses on intelligence techniques, business counterintelligence, and one class entitled "Elicitation and Trade Show/Conference Intelligence Operations." For about $2,000 company executives can spend two days at a trade show and learn the ways of the corporate intelligence officer. The curriculum is based on ethical collection, using skills both DeGenaro and Nolan have turned into high art. But what do they do if they simply can't get the information they need without resorting to subterfuge and a client is breathing down their necks? They do what everyone else seems to do: Ignore those inconvenient SCIP rules, even though they both publicly embrace them.

Nolan, founder of the highly successful Phoenix Consulting Group in Huntsville, Alabama, farms out work to an information broker named Linda Rhea to assist him with intelligence projects. Like most information brokers, Rhea's specialty is illegally acquiring telephone "tolls"—long-distance phone records—as well as credit reports and banking records. Some information brokers have been known to sell a target's medical and psychological records, and even IRS tax returns, for as little as $2,000. Yet in Nolan's 1999 book, *Confidential: Uncover Your Competitors' Top Business Secrets Legally and Quickly—and Protect Your Own*, he writes about what he labels "Windfall Information." For example, two people next to you start talking about business matters, and you realize they work for a competitor.

whether or not they have started to talk about competitively sensitive information, Nolan urges you to "reveal your identity promptly." Given Nolan's actions in the real world, one wonders if he would follow his own advice. DeGenaro has also been known to flout SCIP ethical rules. He has, through third parties, provided copies of a credit report of a CEO who was suspected of circumventing Israeli election laws and funneling money to presidential candidates in Israel. On his office wall, DeGenaro even displays a framed "burn bag," which is used by government attachés and intelligence agents to incinerate confidential papers in a hurry.

Although running tolls and pulling credit reports are standard operating procedure for private detectives, and would make both DeGenaro and Nolan heroes in some circles, these tactics are forbidden in corporate marketing departments. They are also considered major violations of SCIP ethical rules. But these rules are so unrealistic that corporate spooks like Fadel scoff at the silliness of them. Yet despite SCIP's open-source rhetoric, members with a government intelligence background tend to have a nudge, nudge, wink, wink attitude toward the ethical rules. As one French Intelligence expert, who runs a web site dedicated to military and corporate intelligence (a subscription runs about $1,000), says: "Only Americans could be so arrogant as to say, Yes, we spy on our competition, but we do it ethically."

Fadel, on the other hand, has no qualms doing whatever it takes to get the job done. The stepson of a diplomatic correspondent for a major newsmagazine, he moved around a lot growing up, which helps explain his ability to fit in seamlessly, whatever the context. Born in Lebanon, he spent his first seven years in Cairo, five years in the United States, then a couple of years in London. Fadel didn't grow up with James Bond on the brain, nor did he enroll in DeGenaro and Nolan's spy school; he fell into the job completely by accident. He says he was always interested in psychology, and for a long time wanted to study it in college, but realized he didn't want to be a doctor. "Too much work, too much preparation to get there," he says. "I figured I couldn't lose with a degree in business." While an undergraduate student at Boston University, he worked at PictureTel as a temp, then landed an internship. After graduation he was hired to take over "business collection" from his predecessor when a friend of his declined the company's offer. The job description called for an MBA and five years' experience. He had a BA and about a year and a half under his belt.

The month he started his new job in October 1997, the twenty-three-year-old freshly graduated Fadel found himself in the thick of a corporate crisis. "I was slammed from day one," he says. Picture-Tel rival Polycom had just introduced the ViewStation, a product that promised to cause massive migraines for Polycom's competitors. It offered high-end quality and performance at a low price and was the first videoconferencing system to include an embedded web server and web-based integrated presentation system.

With practically no experience or guidance, Fadel had to analyze the ViewStation and run side-by-side test comparisons against his company's products (PictureTel buys all of its competitors' products to dissect). He then had to provide PictureTel's sales force with a clear understanding of how to sell against a clearly superior product. Despite his best efforts, ViewStation took Polycom from a $40 million company to a $130 million company, pushing its market share from zero to an astounding 30 percent within eighteen months. It earned awards at both the CeBit and Telecon trade shows and *Teleconnect* magazine named it "Product of the Year." PictureTel, number one in the videoconferencing market, was feeling the heat. "I was completely lost at first," Fadel says. "The sales force was screaming for positional arguments, but I had to first understand what the business was about. It is very difficult to play catch-up while having to come up with information they could use. I was working fifteen-hour days." This prompted Fadel to double his efforts at bringing in useful intelligence, and that meant hitting the trade shows.

His collection activities don't begin the minute he steps into a conference hall. They start in the days before, when he downloads trade show maps from the Internet so he knows exactly where his targets' booths are situated. (It's not as if companies want to hide.) Fadel has a plethora of fake business cards with the names of fake consultants. On the cards: phony work and home telephone numbers and the address of a friend or relative. Most people don't bother to return calls after a trade show, and he doesn't want someone calling him at random. It's happened a couple of times when he was caught off guard. Fadel usually makes an excuse—"I have another call," he'll say—then begs off, phoning back later and asking for any information to be sent to his home address.

At conventions he wears a badge with a fake name. He always goes by Karim, changing only his last name. That way there are fewer things to remember. Besides, if someone recognizes him from one of the many marketing seminars he gives as part of his job, he can take quick action. "You never know who will show up and call you by your real name and blow your cover," he says. "I haven't slipped up yet but at one trade show I was almost picked out by a guy who works for a PictureTel reseller. I had my badge on with a fake name and company on it. The guy yells across the floor, 'Hey, Karim,' but he used my real last name, not the one on my badge. So I quickly took off the badge and turned around to greet him. That was a close call."

When working a trade show Fadel takes lunch inside the conference hall and seeks targets, eyeing badges while carrying a tray of food, or he will look for someone donning a T-shirt with a competitor's name on it. He doesn't speak to anyone, he merely observes and listens; although people may be on guard at their booths, they are rarely on guard at lunch.

He also pays close attention to conversations held in airports and on airplanes. Places especially rich in business information: departure gates and the baggage claim. And since many conventioneers do their traveling the day before a trade show, Fadel has found himself sitting ahead of people employed by PictureTel competitors. "On an airplane I came across a couple of guys working for VTEL," he says. "They were talking about one of the features on a new product when one of them remarked, 'Oh, it sucks.' At the show I went to some resellers and told them that even people inside VTEL say the product isn't as robust as they would like it to be. The truth is the best weapon, and getting it from the horse's mouth is the ultimate weapon."

VTEL isn't above playing dirty tricks on PictureTel either. Every year PictureTel sponsors a conference in which it invites 500 of its best customers. There the company unveils exhibits, champions new products, exchanges ideas with its top users, and has its partners offer presentations. Members of PictureTel's User Group (PUG) receive special privileges, like first dibs on special promotions. Or if the company is trying to rid itself of excess inventory, it will offer PUG members 50 percent discounts on selected products. At the PUG conference in Sacramento, California, in September 1999, VTEL rented a suite to demonstrate its product line, tacking up all sorts of billboards to direct PictureTel conference goers to its suite. "Guilty as charged," admits Mike Russell, VTEL's senior director of investor relations. Unfortunately for VTEL, the rival conference within a conference backfired when PictureTel users failed to be swayed by this obvious ploy.

One way to find out what a competitor plans to announce at a convention is to cultivate trade journalists, those underpaid, underappreciated reporters who cover an industry from the inside out. The good ones know when a CEO on their beat sneezes, and even when they don't publish something for lack of space or because it is unsubstantiated, they often have access to valuable information. Fadel has a whole host of trade journalists with whom he keeps in regular contact, plying them with drinks and conversation. But he isn't the only one. George Dennis, director of competitor intelligence at Telcordia, a telecommunications company formerly known as Bellcore, says trade journalists are often experts, but not paid nearly as much as those whose activities they cover, and this creates resentment that can be used to your advantage if you exploit their need for respect.

"If I were interested in a particular executive and the journalist interviewed him recently, I would call and ask what he put in the story that the editor took out. Most journalists usually write longer than their stories end up being in print." Sometimes he convinces a trade journalist to write a follow-up story on a topic of interest to him by claiming to be an enthusiastic reader. "The journalist winds up becoming your gofer," he says. And if a story is killed, even better, because then it's possible the reporter, especially over a few drinks, will be more than happy to share his notes. Barry says some spooks maintain a stable of trade journalists they pay on the sly. Once they have them on the payroll, and their credibility is at stake, the spies can manipulate them into conducting interviews and digging up information for a client's benefit.

The boldest info scam Fadel himself has ever pulled off at a trade show was against Lucent Technologies, a conglomerate sprawled across Murray Hill, New Jersey, that is both a PictureTel competitor and reseller of various brands. The videoconferencing market is teeming with such conflicts, in which competitors can be partners and vice versa. For instance, Lucent resells PictureTel products in the United States and also distributes Polycom ViewStations. It is a sticky situation, one that Fadel, who has given countless demos to the company, fully mines to his advantage.

"I can spy on one of our competitors by spying on a reseller: Lucent," he says. "That way I am actually spying on Polycom." Or he can go the direct route and gather intelligence on Lucent. Either way, he does it at the Lucent booth, a one-stop shop for data diggers. Lucent, spun off from telecommunications papa AT&T in September 1996, is North America's leading maker of telecom equipment and software. Through a series of clever acquisitions it has also leveraged its broadband business, quickly becoming a force in videoconferencing. Although PictureTel, selling its products almost exclusively through resellers and distributors, is dependent on Lucent, it also competes against it. If PictureTel is to stay ahead, Fadel needs to know what the $165 billion tech conglomerate, with almost 500 times the market capitalization of PictureTel, is up to. In 1998, Lucent announced it was producing a high-end multipoint control unit, or MCU, which allows up to thirty sites on one connection and brings in margins as high as 70 percent. Fadel hit CeBIT to find out more.

Playing a London-based consultant advising Global 500 companies on network and multimedia compatibility, Fadel traveled to Hannover, Germany. Costumed in standard-issue slacks and a button-down shirt (he dresses fashionably only when he pretends to be a market analyst), he approached Lucent and employed his standard spying operating procedure. He told the reps he was working on a big deal for a client in New York City that was looking at several vendors' equipment, including Lucent's. He was whisked upstairs to an elegant European-style café, where about 100 people were brokering deals and noshing on fine food. From the posh balcony Fadel could see almost the entire trade floor.

Over chocolate croissants and coffee, Fadel informed the Lucent rep that his client, who he was not at liberty to name, was looking to install an MCU worth about $200,000 to connect multiple offices around the world, and he was recommending Lucent. "I also mentioned PictureTel, but said I didn't like to deal with them," Fadel says. "'I'm sick and tired of dealing with these people. They are not responsive to their customers. I'd rather deal with you guys at Lucent. You have a good reputation.' The guy was honored and laughed. That's when I knew I had him."

Then Fadel handed the rep a list of specifications based on three separate configurations that PictureTel itself offers; that way he could get a pure side-by-side price comparison between Lucent's product and PictureTel's. Fadel told him he needed high-speed and data-sharing capacity, plus speed matching, a piece of hardware that allows different rates of speed to be connected smoothly. The higher the speed, the more bandwidth, the more expensive. "I told the guy I needed this ASAP and the next day he came back with three different price quotes based on the three different configurations I requested," Fadel says. "A month later I called him and said, 'Look, the client chose another company. It was a political situation. Some guy knew some guy, but I really appreciate the trouble you went to.' That way I got to keep him as a contact."

Fadel's job doesn't only encompass targeting competitors for information. He is also responsible for parrying rivals' attempts at sabotaging PictureTel, particularly those of Polycom, which Fadel claims has targeted PictureTel since its inception in 1990. There is bad blood between the two video phone firms, mostly owing to the fact that the same man created both: Brian Hinman, a founder of PictureTel and vice president of engineering and a director from 1984 through 1990, who, in a huff, took his expertise to upstart start-up Polycom.

In 1999, a week before PictureTel was scheduled to have a partners' conference in Boston for its yearly feel-good meeting, Polycom posted an ambiguous message on its web site, bragging that it "changed the teleconferencing industry forever with ViewStation. . . . On April 19th, we will do it again." It was no coincidence that

April 19 was the same day PictureTel was having its conference. As a result, Polycom shares shot up 16 percent one day, then 29 percent the next, after an analyst, pointing to the web site message, predicted that the company would announce an Internet-based product. Fadel had two days to find out what Polycom's secret was and concoct a strategy to short-circuit it.

The first thing Fadel did was phone one of his many former PictureTel comrades who had joined with the enemy, a man who worked in sales for both companies. They hadn't spoken since Fadel had left London and relocated to Andover, Massachusetts, when they had gone out for a long night of drinking. "'Hey, how are you?'" Fadel asks. "'How's Polycom treating you?' Of course he knew why I was calling. 'Come on, out with it, Karim,' he said. So I go fishing. I tell him I hear Polycom has an integrated streaming product, that it's a low-end system, and there are partnerships. 'Well,' he says, 'I can't tell you exactly, but it's none of the above. You are on the right track but not hitting it on the head.'"

Now all Fadel had to do was call someone else he did business with, a Polycom reseller from whom Fadel had once bought a ViewStation to take apart and study in-house. Since there is something about making an international call that makes people want to talk more, he dialed England instead of a source in the States. Fadel started off by telling his contact about some organizational changes PictureTel was making, nothing confidential but enough to give the illusion he was sharing key information. "You have to give a little to get a little," he says. "Then I told him I knew Polycom was going to make an announcement on April 19, and I needed to confirm the rumors. He said, I hear they are coming out with a sub-$4,000 ViewStation." At the conference, Fadel timed his presentation to begin five minutes after Polycom's highly hyped announcement, blistering the new product and spinning the media: "'It runs at low bandwidth,' I said, 'which makes it a low-quality product. It's like buying a Radio Shack small boombox versus a high-end stereo with integrated components that offer extremely high fidelity.'" Fadel had supplied PictureTel's executives with talking points. As a result, Polycom's stock price actually dipped $5.

But this was a short victory dance for PictureTel. Despite Fadel's best efforts, PictureTel is a company in disarray, its stock price scraping bottom, its market share imploding. Once the industry leader with a brand name synonymous with videoconferencing technology, it is presently number two and falling, its management team in disarray, its skilled engineers, designers, and salespeople leaving in droves. Now Polycom is number one in the market by twenty points, and companies that have been able to incorporate the Internet into its products, despite narrow bandwidth, are on the verge of passing PictureTel. Fadel himself plans to leave as well, having accepted a position with a new company in a new industry, where he will concentrate more on overall strategy and less on collecting competitor information.

As for his business-is-war stratagems: "I have no regrets over what I've done, only the fact that we couldn't win."

6

Spy Trap–P. Y. Yang

The arrest of the then-seventy-one-year-old Yang and his thirty-nine-year-old daughter at Cleveland Hopkins International Airport in September 1997 prompted a media squall in Taiwan, where Chinese-language newspapers fronted the story for several days. In what must have been a gut-curling experience, both Yangs were locked up in the Lake County and Cuyahoga County jails while a federal grand jury indicted them for fraud, money laundering, possession of stolen property, and violation of the economic espionage law.

Wholly ignorant of the American legal system, they each retained legal counsel. P. Y. Yang, acting on advice from friends, hired a former prosecutor, Patrick M. McLauglin of Cleveland; Sally Yang also stayed local with her choice, Ralph E. Cascarilla. Eleven days into their jailhouse captivity, their lawyers got the Yangs a preliminary hearing to determine whether they would be freed on bond or held for trial, and whether there had been probable cause in the first place for their case to be sent to a grand jury. For two days of hearings, the lawyers attempted to show that the government's case rested precariously on biased sources: Ten Hong (Victor) Lee, a man forced to work against the Yangs to save his own hide, and Avery Dennison, an arch rival to the Yangs' Four Pillars Enterprise Co. Ltd.

Judge David S. Perelman, over the strenuous objections of Department of Justice attorney Toren, decided to grant bail. He ruled that the Yangs could be released on unsecured $500,000 bonds and placed under house arrest. As a surety on the bond, Four Pillars put up a 265-acre spread of land it owned in Houston as collateral.

"If I locked up everybody with the potential or intent not to come back, nearly everyone who appears before me would be in detention," Judge Perelman said. He did, however, order the Yangs to surrender their passports and don electronic monitoring devices around their ankles. In addition, their phone calls would be monitored.

Ralph Cascarilla, Sally Yang's attorney, hoped the judge would rule that the government didn't have enough probable cause to have set up the sting in the first place. After the Yangs received bail, winning round one, he said, "We have raised serious concerns about the government's accusations. This case has been aired as a commercial dispute between two companies." But the Yangs lost that battle and moved into their new digs: adjoining apartments separated by a single lockable door.

The Yang's motel-drab digs were furnished with court-bought furniture that appeared slightly too large. Neither Sally nor P. Y. Yang had much in the way of personal effects, and since the government would not guarantee it would refrain from arresting visiting relatives or Four Pillars employees, they were cut off from their friends and family, including P. Y. Yang's ninety-six-year-old mother and newborn granddaughter. Since his arrest it had been impossible for Yang to run his company. He had already decided that because of his age and health, and the disgrace his arrest had brought him, he would step down from overseeing Four Pillars upon his return to Taiwan.

He just wished he had paid more attention to the material Lee had turned over to Four Pillars. In their initial discussions Yang had merely requested that Lee function as Four Pillars' eyes and ears in the States. Yang hadn't known what to expect from the Avery scientist when he hired him all those years ago. He figured anything Lee came up with would justify the investment. He claims he half-expected Lee to satisfy his obligations by mailing over dusty library books, newspaper clippings, and the occasional market study.

Yang must have been pleasantly surprised, then, when Lee mailed him adhesive formulas, master curves—sticky substance blueprints—software that Lee himself had coded, test comparisons between Avery and Four Pillars products, and research papers that his daughter Sally, a research chemist, understood but that he found impenetrable. He didn't pretend to be a scientist. He was a salesman; that's what he was good at, and that's how he had built the company—by leaving the science to others. This is why he had decreed that Four Pillars plow 3.5 percent of total sales into research and development, which sounded like a lot until you compared it with Avery Dennison's R&D.

Four Pillars owed its existence to septuagenarian P. Y. Yang, who had built his company from the muddy ground up. Although spare and slight in appearance and battling nasal cancer, Yang was imbued with the inner toughness to successfully outmaneuver competitors until all that remained were Four Pillars and a lone competitor, Kao Kuan, which had half of Four Pillars' share of the tacky-tape market. Born in Occupied Japan, Yang had started Four Pillars in 1954 with a few partners and a few hundred dollars.

In the company's lean early days he rode around Taipei on a bicycle, selling household tape, the company's sole product at the time, door to door. Proud of his success, Yang remained active in the company's day-to-day operations, believing a leader should understand its inner workings. As Four Pillars grew into the largest sticky-tape maker in Taiwan, adding new products and technologies, he took it upon himself to learn all about his company's manufacturing processes, working in his own factories for a time and contracting nasal cancer in 1982, which his doctors believe can be traced to his own plants' toxicity.

Yang claims he felt he himself was the real victim. He firmly believed Avery had stolen from him. During joint venture discussions, against the wishes of some of his advisers, Yang had provided Avery with key product information, as well as financial information going back many years. That had been a big mistake. Now he believed Avery had never been interested in joining forces with him. And alone, Yang was vulnerable in Asia. "Four Pillars cannot compete with a business of the size and power of Avery," he admitted.

When Lee told him about Avery's patent application, Yang knew he would need a copy to pass on to his lawyers back in Taiwan. This is why he took the documents from Lee. He believed the patent was for a formula similar to a Four Pillars adhesive. He asked himself, Was Avery Dennison violating Four Pillars' patent rights? Could Avery turn around and brazenly use this patent against him by accusing Four Pillars of infringing on its own patent?

But the least ethical part of the FBI-Avery sting was the use of the Asian expansion plan, Yang believed, because it included a section on Avery's plan to "steal" a Four Pillars scientist. They show him this months after Yang almost loses Guo to Avery? But he knew the videotape of the hotel sting, of him cutting off the "CONFIDENTIAL" blocks from Avery's documents—something Yang would call "my instinctive reaction" because he was so worried and not thinking clearly—was damning. Yang had simply wanted to show Avery's patent application to a lawyer in Taiwan and didn't want to get hassled on his way out of the country.

After moving into his spare apartment his case hit a snag. Although his attorney, McLauglin, pressed him to plea, the government and Avery played hardball over the discovery process. In most cases, the defense would move to gain access to all of the evidence amassed against his client, since a defense attorney can't work a case until he has gotten discovery. But Avery was claiming that the evidence contained information that was confidential to Avery Dennison, and it would be potentially harmful to the company if the defense were to show this information to outside experts, many of whom work as industry consultants for Avery competitors. The biggest problem Yang had with a plea bargain was that he would be ceding victory to Avery in the civil case, opening Four Pillars up to almost unlimited liability. Yang would later say he made errors in judgment but that he hadn't broken the law, and he didn't want his company to suffer for any mistakes he had made.

When Yang finally comprehended the terms of the plea agreement that his attorney recommended he sign, he became angry. He believed Avery was the cause of all his troubles. It had used joint venture talks as a cover to cull vital technology from Yang's company. It had then patented Four Pillars technology and used that and a fake business plan to lure him to America. In the Asian expansion plan there was a section on targeting key Four Pillars employees to gain access to Four Pillars technology, which is what Avery had tried to do with Guo, according to Yang. And from his now four-wall perspective, what happens when he goes to America to liberate his own technology and gather evidence of Avery targeting his employees? He ends up being the one arrested and threatened with jail. If Yang was going down, he was going down fighting. He fired McLauglin and started looking for a new attorney who would stand up to Avery.

Yang contacted friends in Taiwan and the same name kept being tossed back at him: Nancy A. Luque of the Washington, D.C.,

firm Reed Smith Shaw & McClay. Luque, a white-collar defense attorney, had been defending Maria Hsia, a Los Angeles immigration
consultant charged with arranging more than $100,000 in illegal
donations during the 1996 presidential campaign, a case that had
been receiving ample press coverage in Taiwan, since Hsia had
roots there.

One of Yang's friends in Taiwan told him about something the
papers reported Luque had said, taking the entire Asian American
community to task for not coming to the aid of Hsia, a fellow
Asian. This wouldn't happen in the black or Hispanic communities, Luque had said. You need to stand up. And Yang knew he had
found his attorney.

Forty-two years old, "hair brown by artifice," Luque uses words
like "passionate," "emotional," and "stubborn" to describe herself.
She says she views the courtroom as a battlefield, the prosecution
as the enemy. After graduating from the University of San Diego
law school, she interned at the district attorney's office in San
Diego and prosecuted cases in the Sacramento DA's office. But after working cases involving serial murder and child abuse, she lost
the desire to be a prosecutor and switched to public interest law,
swinging over to Jerry Brown. In 1979 she moved to Washington,
D.C., to work for the Department of Justice antitrust division, but
that didn't last either.

Luque bounced over to the U.S. Attorneys Office, where she
eventually accepted a position as supervisor in the grand jury section, the perfect job, or so she thought. She says: "I got to talk
Fourth Amendment violations. I decided what got indicted, what
got pursued. I had found my niche." Then her boss, Jay Stephens,
designed a sting operation to nail Mayor Marion Barry smoking
crack and Luque decided she didn't want to work there anymore.
"I didn't believe the office had integrity anymore," she says. She
morphed once again, becoming a defense attorney specializing in

white-collar crime and became a partner at Reed Smith Shaw & McClay in 1995.

Four Pillars in Taiwan contacted Luque while she was in the midst of a major media brouhaha with Whitewater and Monicagate special prosecutor Ken Starr over Luque's client, Julie Hiatt Steele, who, like legions of others, had been accused of obstructing justice by the special prosecutor.

The minute Luque saw Yang, she says her heart shook. Here was this frail old man with sagebrush-sparse gray hair. She could see he'd had trouble getting his trouser leg over the lumpy, black ankle bracelet he was forced to wear. And his daughter Sally, "she's beautiful, dark hair and dimples," Luque says. They lived as if they didn't wish to leave an imprint, their apartments spare and impersonal. A woman who did not mind letting her emotions dictate her actions, Luque immediately connected with the Yangs.

"You couldn't talk to P. Y. without feeling fondness for him," she says. "And can you imagine if it were reversed? What would an American CEO do if he were locked up in a Taiwanese jail?"

Yang debriefed Luque on the situation, telling her about Lee, the joint venture talks with Avery that had gone awry, the battle over Guo, the sting operation, the patent he thought he had been retrieving, his arrest, and the plea agreements he had spurned. Four Pillars hired Lee to be its eyes and ears in the United States, he said. He expected books, articles, and other publicly accessible material, a necessary component of research in those pre-Internet days. As she listened, Luque wondered how the material could be so confidential and secret if a low-ling like Lee had access to it? He was a research assistant and tested products. He could not have had access to trade secrets. If he had, it's Avery's fault, since they didn't have adequate policies in place to protect them.

Luque realized Avery was gaining a tremendous economic advantage from the Department of Justice's pursuit of the case, holding the leader of a competitor captive in the United States as the trial proceedings, and the trial itself, dragged on. While P. Y. Yang, the heart, soul and founder of Four Pillars, spent two years under house arrest in an apartment in Ohio, Avery made a mad dash into the Asian market. It put up factories and distribution channels in China and watched its sales there grow 35 percent a year while Four Pillars treaded water, waiting for the case to be resolved and Yang, the company's leader, to come home.

Working with the Department of Justice, which was endeavoring to send a message to would-be corporate spies, Avery, Luque believed, consciously or not, was capitalizing on the EEA, using it as a way to gain a competitive advantage over a rival preeminent in a region Avery wished to exploit. "When you get down to it, Avery used the government to crush a competitor in Asia," she says.

Avery had been searching for ways to decapitate the Taiwanese tape maker well before the two companies had entered joint venture talks in the early 1990s, a venture Yang concluded Avery had no intention of pursuing. Instead, during two-plus years of negotiation, Four Pillars opened its door to Avery, allowing it to gain access to its manufacturing processes, including one for a universal adhesive created from a few chemicals instead of the dozens—sometimes hundreds—that Avery had to mishmash together for a similar product. "This is why P. Y. Yang came to America: to get the patent back," Luque says, "and you can't steal your own product."

As Luque listened her sense of outrage grew. The two defense attorneys believed right away that the law had been misapplied in the Yangs' case. In their mind prosecutors had jumped at an opportunity to participate in the first court test of the Economic Espionage Act without exploring the merits of their case. Judging by the way the government had indicted the case, Luque and Dubelier knew they would be able to whittle down most of the twenty-one counts in the indictment, many relating to wire and mail fraud, with two counts tied to money laundering, and two more relating to the Economic Espionage Act.

Since most of Lee's activities had occurred in the early years of their relationship, the statute of limitations would work in their favor. The most troublesome piece of evidence was not Lee's copious notes. He could be impeached—he was a flipper who had turned at the first sight of governmental authority and coerced into testifying in Avery's favor by his former employers. No, Lee would be meat on the witness stand. It was the videotape. That was the one piece of evidence that could send the Yangs to prison. But there was a chance they could persuade a judge to dismiss it as evidence if they could show that the FBI had relied on tainted evidence. The patent was something Yang thought Four Pillars might own. The bogus business plan that cited (in bold) Four Pillars as a top place to raid for scientific talent was entrapment, coming on the heels of the Guo debacle.

Luque looked over at Dubelier and each knew right there and then they would take the case. But one thing, Luque told Yang. She would fight for him, but "there is no way you are going to jail on my watch. If you want to plea bargain I'm the wrong attorney for you."

Yang smiled for the first time in a year. It was exactly what he wanted to hear.

7

The Librarian

Liz Lightfoot sits in her cubicle at Teltech, a mid-size information resource company in Minneapolis, Minnesota. All around her are other "veal chambers," crisscrossing in rows and gussied up with white walls and drab institutional carpeting. But Lightfoot likes the latticelike architecture. "It keeps me in the stream of things," she says.

Through her window she can see the Mall of America, a mammoth structure the color of scraped concrete and almost epic in its ugliness. Locals tout it as the largest indoor shopping center in the world, a magnet for Europeans who fly to Minnesota for the day to bargain shop, cram their purchases into airplane baggage holds and overhead compartments, then get liquored up for the flight home. A former chemical industry research consultant, Lightfoot and 100 or so other Teltech research analysts gather and synthesize information for a living. Using "open source" collection techniques, "no fake identities or pretext calls," she swears, Teltech has performed projects for more than half of the Fortune 500 corporations, including AlliedSignal, BASF, Caterpillar, Deere & Co., General Electric, Lockheed Martin, Owens Corning, TRW, and Warner-

Lambert. Although Garrison Keillor's fictional town of Lake Woebegone may be the place where "all the children are above average," Teltech staff are downright brainy.

Teltech isn't the only company to reap the rewards of this informational bonanza. There are a number of corporate intelligence firms, such as Boston-based Fuld & Co.; Kirk Tyson International of Lisle, Illinois; Strategic Analysis, which, like Teltech, calls Minneapolis home; large consultancies, like Ernst & Young; international detective agencies, like Kroll Associates; and dozens of small one- and two-man operations. There are also the information brokers that troll the seamy side of cyberspace: Dig Dirt Inc., Infoseekers.com, and Docusearch.com all offer services à la carte.

Docusearch, for example, will get a client your unlisted bank balances for $45, your phone number or Social Security number for $49, or your driving record for $35. Tracing a cell phone number will set you back $84, and the company can even find out what stocks, bonds, and securities you possess ($209). For added convenience Docusearch has an Amazonlike shopping cart function coded into its web site. Click on what you want, input your credit card number, and expect results in a few days. Docusearch's founder, Daniel Cohn, has a PI license from the state of Florida, which he claims allows him to use pretext to glean personal information. Often he will pose as the target or the target's spouse and dupe customer service representatives into passing him the data he needs. Or he will say, "Hi, I'm Dan Cohn, a state-licensed investigator doing an investigation," knowing the words "state-licensed investigator" make it sound like he is sanctioned by law enforcement.

Lightfoot, on the other hand, claims she can get everything she needs without resorting to such trickery, believing that sheer laziness and a lack of know-how compel companies to cross the line. She has a term for people who do: lawbreakers. Hardened spooks such as Barry, DeGenaro, and Nolan have a word for people like her, too. They derisively call them "librarians." But that doesn't mean that everyone subsumed under this category is as scrupulous as Lightfoot. Many of the information resource companies advertise themselves as open-source collectors, but not everyone plays by the rules. Strategic Analysis was once accused of collecting information on one of its own clients, 3M, then turning over the data to Norton, an arch enemy from France. Kroll outsources much of its work, so it doesn't know whether information culled on behalf of a client has been collected ethically or not. And when the going gets tough, many open-source data collectors turn to the information brokers, who will stop at nothing to get what their clients demand.

Teltech's services run the gamut. Its rates start at $25,000 for a year of basic research (a kind of help line for companies that need quick answers to technical questions) and range above $1 million for large projects. The Internet, which has given researchers easy access to data that was unthinkable just a few years ago, has been indispensable to the company's growth. Bioanalytic Microsystems, a startup out of the University of Minnesota, hired Teltech to gauge interest in a prostate cancer therapy that might improve delivery of radioactive seeds used in lieu of surgery. Minnesota Valley Engineering retained the firm to locate a niche for a new type of industrial pipe.

Since Disney has such a large and loyal following, one of its entertainment rivals asked Teltech to use the Internet to keep tabs on the mighty Mouse, since many of its fans post news and inside information on web sites. And Teltech monitors chat rooms for a Fortune 500 cosmetics company keen on finding out what consumers really think of its products and those of its competitors. That way its client receives unvarnished views not available from traditional market research groups. "A decade ago the problem companies had was access to information," says Teltech president Andrew Michuda, a Minnesotan who brings to mind Craig T. Nelson, star of the old ABC sitcom *Coach*. "But with the Internet, now the problem is info glut—how do you make sense of all the information out there?"

This time Lightfoot's assignment would come from Dow Chemical, the world's second largest chemical company (after DuPont), which earned $18 billion in annual sales and known for making the plastics and chemicals that underlie (some might say undermine) life. "We don't supply a finished dashboard of a car to the Ford Motor corporation," Dr. William Dowd, a Dow research director, says. "We supply the materials to the people who make this dashboard for Ford." Dow R&D had uncovered the magical mysteries of styrofoam and Saran Wrap; it had also given the world Agent Orange, napalm, and silicone breast implants, and it continued selling the pesticide DBCP abroad even after it had been banned in the United States because of fears that it caused sterility.

In August 1999, the company merged with another chemical juggernaut, also with a checkered past: Union Carbide. Makers of household icons like Eveready batteries and Glad plastic bags, Union Carbide was responsible for the 1984 chemical gas leak in Bhopal, India, that caused as many as 10,000 exposure-related deaths and injured 200,000 people. Lightfoot had started her research before the Union Carbide merger, and besides, she never concerned herself with a client's past. If she did, she might not have any clients. Truth be told, all she cared about was finding as much as she could about a new type of heat-resistant, super-strong composite in the R&D phase. The new plastic had the potential to go where no plastic had gone before, as a replacement for metal or steel, under the hoods of cars in superhot engines or on snowplows in Alaskan winters, introduced as a replacement for polyethylene terephthalate (PET) in plastic bottles, or used in disposable, microwaveable containers. But before committing money from its $800 million-a-year research budget, Dow needed to know two things: Was there a market for this new plastic? And was any rival already too far ahead?

Dow would learn far more than that. Lightfoot had been given the assignment because she spoke the language of science and was known for her tenacity. Her nickname at Teltech was "Rat Killer," inscribed in a plaque glued to the outside of her cubicle. She had gotten the Rat Killer tag from her days in graduate school, where she was studying toxicology. Her research required rat liver enzymes and the only way to harvest them was fresh from the animal: "I'd pick the rats up by the tail and swing them to disorient them, then snap their heads on the lab bench," Lightfoot says with insouciance. "After they were knocked unconscious, I'd stick them in a guillotine and cut their little heads off."

Eventually she developed an allergy to lab rats and moved to the paper side of the chemical business. But science wasn't her first career choice. She had met her first husband in high school (about that she says, "I think God must have a sense of humor") but within a few short years was divorced, alone, and caring for a child. Lightfoot, who kept her first husband's name because it has a better ring than "Liz Brown," had wanted to be a Broadway singer; instead she was a young single mom in the early 1970s. She decided to give nursing a try but after taking a test was told she had special abilities and should go to college.

Starting with junior college courses, Lightfoot eventually received a master's in science and environmental health at Wayne State University in Michigan and took a job as a chemical industry researcher for Ethyl Corporation in Richmond, Virginia, where she worked for thirteen years. When her second husband was transferred to Minnesota, she took the job at Teltech, where she wound her way up to manager of in-depth research services. The forty-five-year-old Lightfoot had been at Teltech for four years before starting the Dow project and had gotten to the point that all that she would need for her three-month reconnaissance was a comfortable chair, a computer with web access, and a telephone, the stock tools of her trade.

Dow had supplied her with a list of questions about "nanocomposites," materials constructed by tightly packing together particles of two or more materials. Dow was most interested in clay and polymer blends. If the company could perfect the technology and manufacture it at a reasonable cost, then it could capture a significant chunk of a market worth hundreds of millions of dollars. But first it had to understand the competitive landscape. "Everything we do is cost-driven," Dr. Dowd says. "We could make you almost anything you want if you are willing to pay for it. But if you only project the value to a customer without having an idea how much he will pay, or don't know what the competitors are doing, you will probably be very disappointed."

One place Dow knew it could make major inroads was in the automobile industry, which depends a great deal on polypropylene, a plastic Dow and its rivals produce in large quantities that is often used in car interiors. If Chrysler, Ford, or GM were to construct a door panel out of polypro, it would be fine in the Arizona sun, but if you slammed it shut in Minnesota cold it might shatter. If an additive were mixed with the polypropylene so that it could handle colder temperatures, it would lose its ability to withstand high temperatures. But nanocomposites had the potential to function on both the high and low ends of the temperature spectrum. "You go to GM and say we have a product that meets all your needs so you don't have to recycle four types of plastics," Dr. Dowd says. "It would save time, save money, and the engineer would only have to understand one type of material, not four."

Another potentially lucrative market: soda pop and perhaps even beer bottles. Have you ever wondered why you can buy a plastic bottle of Coke in stores, but only in twenty-ounce sizes or larger? That's because they are made out of PET, which, because of its surface to volume in smaller sizes, leaks carbon dioxide—the stuff that gives cola its fizz—through the sides of the bottles. But the molecules in nanocomposites are crammed closer together and can slow down the migration of CO_2. Nanocomposites would have the longer shelf life of two-liter PET bottles but could be made available in popular twelve-ounce sizes. It would also dovetail well with America's culture of convenience. Since nanocomposites can withstand severe changes in temperature, it would be perfect as a container for frozen food that could be zapped in a microwave and served piping hot right off its own plate. But just because it seemed like a great idea in the lab didn't mean Dow should go through the time and expense of creating a product for the marketplace. "Teltech could have told us two things that would have put an immediate end to our R&D," Dr. Dowd says. "There is no market for the product, or that it is a great idea but we are five years too late because our competition is about to release a product. Without Teltech it would have taken a lot more time and cost us a lot more money to find this out on our own." What would have been the worst case scenario? he was asked. If Teltech had discovered that a competitor was going to release a product within a year and a half. "If it were six months," Dowd says, "I like to think we would have known that. But if it were eighteen months, we probably wouldn't have known."

Over the years, Lightfoot had developed a research strategy she calls the "bull's-eye method": Start at the outer rings and work inward toward your target. Since she started out knowing very little about nanocomposites, she jumped on the Internet and plugged in various related terms, like "nano-particles," "nano technologies,"

and "nanocomposites," plus "clay" and "polymer" into Dow Jones
News Service, as well as accessing a bunch of other databases related to science, technology, and patents. She did the same with Internet search engines Alta Vista, Lycos, and HotBot, since each
spits out slightly different results. Since Dow wanted to know
where the nanocomposite technology was in terms of development
cycle, especially as it related to compounds produced from clay
and polymers—was it still in the university lab phase? Were companies already trying to create products out of it?—Lightfoot had to
cast a wide net. "First you have to get smart so you can ask intelli-
gent questions," she says. "Typically you're looking for market information, trade and technical literature, and patents through the
various databases, and on the Internet you check for research institutes and consortiums. With databases, only the newsworthy stuff
is in them; if it's not newsworthy, it's not there. If I want to find
out about polypropylene on computers, it's in the trade and industry databases. But if it's a new technology, it's probably not there,
but you still have to try."

All told, she amassed about 2,000 pages she printed right off the
Internet. What she found was that the prefix "nano" is deployed in
a variety of ways: It is a term used in electron microscopy, electronic fireworks firing systems, lithography, and even Chinese traditional martial and healing arts. Nanotechnology is the science of
building tools at the submolecular level; nanocomputers are
atomic-scale mechanical computers; nano-size metal particles are
incorporated into electromagnetic applications; nano whiskers are
part of metallurgy. Nano also stands for the Nechako Access Network Organization, a not-for-profit online community in British
Columbia, Canada; it is used as slang in certain cybercircles ("Be
with you in a nano," short for nanosecond); and *The Nano Flower* is
the title of a Star Wars–themed painting available over the Internet.
If "nano" wasn't bad enough, "clay" was even worse. There were

upward of a million items related to clay. After all this reading, however, which took about two weeks, she realized that except for one article there wasn't much out there about nanocomposites made from clay-polymer mixtures. But this didn't mean Lightfoot's Internet search hadn't been fruitful. "The most important thing is getting the names of people working in a related field or technology you can call up," she says. "Before the Internet this would have been a lot harder."

The father of nanotechnology is the late Nobel Laureate physicist Dr. Richard P. Feynman, who in a 1959 speech entitled "Atoms in a Small World" given at the California Institute of Technology, declared that there was plenty of room for technological advancement at the bottom. In essence, he was saying, Think small: "Atoms on a small scale behave like nothing on a large scale, for they satisfy the laws of quantum mechanics," he said. "So, as we go down and fiddle around with the atoms down there, we are working with different laws, and we can expect to do different things. We can manufacture in different ways ... if we go down far enough, all of our devices can be mass produced so that they are absolutely perfect copies of one another." Feynman went on to offer a $1,000 prize out of his own pocket to the first person to take the information on the page of a book and "put it on an area 1/25,000 smaller in linear scale in such manner that it can be read by an electron microscope"—the scale required to publish the *Encyclopaedia Britannica* on the head of a pin. He also promised an additional $1,000 to whoever could create a rotating electric motor that could be controlled from the outside and, not counting the lead-in wires, was only a 1/64-inch cube. Proving that even geniuses are fallible, Feynman had set the size limits slightly too large, and the motor prize was claimed a year later by an engineer who had created a tiny motor that ran on conventional mechanics. (Disappointed, Feynman ponied up the prize anyway.) It was fifteen more years before Feynman had to shell out $1,000 again, to Thomas Newman, a Stanford University graduate student. Using electron beam lithography, he reproduced page one of Charles Dickens's *A Tale of Two Cities* on a sheet measuring only 1/160 millimeter—twenty times smaller than the human eye can see. Since Newman had produced a true technological breakthrough, Feynman gladly paid up.

Today, the Feynman Grand Prize is worth a quarter of a million dollars, to be awarded to the first individual or group to design and construct a functional nanometer-scale robotic arm with specified performance characteristics, and a functional nanometer-scale computing device capable of adding two eight-bit binary numbers. The whole idea behind nanotechnology is that molecules and atoms can be assembled into precise structures. Nano disciples believe the technology will someday allow the construction of supercomputers the size of a sugar cube, pollution-free manufacturing, and molecular-scale robots that could repair damage in individual human cells, with one billion nanorobots able to fit inside a single drop of blood. But Dow Chemical's needs were less sci-fi and more prosaic. The company would be happy if its R&D researchers could find a way to make nanocomposite clay compatible with polymers. "When you put the stuff together, it doesn't spread evenly, so it clumps," Dowd admits. "It doesn't stick to the organic polymers. And for it to work it has to be uniformly distributed over the polymer." But that wasn't Lightfoot's problem. Her job was to find out who was trying to take Feynman's vision into the realm of plastics.

In one of the sci-tech databases Lightfoot had come across in her reading was an article entitled "The Chemistry of Polymer-Clay Hybrids," by Akane Okada and Arimitsu Usuki of the Toyota Central Research and Development Labs of Japan. This told her that someone in the industry was working on the very same issue her client was interested in. The article claimed that the clay polymer had higher performance and could be used to make molded auto parts, and the authors even mentioned the existence of a successful prototype for a timing belt cover, which determines the rotation of the camshaft. Lightfoot, aware that Toyota wasn't in the plastics industry, set out to find out who supplied the clay hybrid for the experiment but came up empty. So she dug through a computerized list of consultants Teltech kept on file and contacted Dr. Fred Ancker, a former Union Carbide engineer who lived in Tarrytown, New York. After telling him what she needed, she began phase two of the project: real, live, breathing sources. "After you've read all you can, you start with a test interview," Lightfoot says. "You have a knowledge base from which to draw. You think you understand the components of the technology. You have some idea of its potential applications: Why would someone use this? What benefit does it have? Now it's time to put this into action. But you need to practice first on a source on the outer ring of the bull's-eye, in case you blow it. Because the closer you get to the center of the bull's-eye, the higher the stakes."

One of Lightfoot's first calls was to Thomas Pinnavaia of Michigan State, an academic with a patent in nanocomposite technology. She kicked off the conversation the same way she always did: "Hello, this is Liz Lightfoot of Teltech." In her four years on the job rarely had anyone asked her what Teltech was and only once had someone known what Teltech did. Pinnavaia wouldn't tell her who was sponsoring his work, but she poked around and found out that one of his projects was funded by the Michigan Materials and Processing Institute (MMPI), an organization supported by key automobile and chemical industry players in materials processing. MMPI wouldn't discuss details but told her Pinnavaia's research was funded by Nanocor, Inc., at the time one of three suppliers of "nanoclay," the nanoparticles that would be combined with the resin/plastic to form the nanocomposite. Lightfoot, feeling she was on to something, cold-called Nanocor and asked to speak to someone technically knowledgeable about its clay products. She was patched through to the company's technical director.

Lightfoot told him the truth: She was doing research for a major chemical company that wanted to determine whether its long-range R&D should include working in the area of nanocomposite technology. "This was my pitch during this whole project, low-key and long-range interest," she says. "Interestingly, no matter what part of the bull's-eye I was in, this information didn't stop people from talking to me, whether they were competitors or not." Nanocor's technical director confirmed it was supporting this professor's research and that its program was being managed by MMPI. He also said that all the resin producers, which supply the raw material for plastic, were trying to be the first to market with commercial products based on nanocomposite technology, and that he was pretty sure AlliedSignal and GE were involved with this type of research but wasn't positive. "Nanocor is working with all the top resin producers in thermoplastic polypropylene," he said.

"Which companies?" Lightfoot asked offhandedly.

"I can't tell you, but I'm certain we are already working with your client, which is. . . ?"

"I'm not at liberty to say."

Stalemate. The truth was Lightfoot didn't know whether Dow was working with Nanocor or not, but that wasn't important. She had been hired to assess the competitive landscape. Sometimes she didn't even know who her client was. But that didn't stop her from doing her job. Now that she knew that resin companies had begun to look at nanocomposites, she waded back into her stack of research and looked for patents or other indicators that would help her narrow the field. There were dozens of resin companies from all over the world, including AlliedSignal, BASF, Bayer, DuPont, Eastman, GE, and Mitsubishi Chemical America, Inc. She narrowed her search somewhat by calling the companies that had filed patents on nanocomposites or on clay-polymer blends and asked them point-blank whether they were looking into the automobile, beverage, and food markets. She paid close attention to corporations already supplying resin to those industries, which were Dow's primary targets, since this meant they already had well-established distribution channels. Leveraging her information, Lightfoot broadened her attack and contacted polypropylene makers and chemical companies—Dow competitors—and, just to cover all of her bases, oil companies. She discovered that AlliedSignal and Eastman Chemicals had implemented research programs centered around clay-polymer nanocomposites and also had an interest in the automobile and beverage markets. In addition, Fina, an oil company, Montel, the world's largest polypropylene maker, and Imperial Chemicals Industries, from Britain, one of the world's largest chemical companies, were all doing research into clay-polymer blends. But she could not find any indication that any of them had been able to create a prototype as Toyota had. Like Dow, they were far from having a product they could market.

"A lot of the companies were aware of it but wouldn't say whether they had programs," Lightfoot says. "I'd rate them whether they had a high awareness, medium amount, or low awareness. There seemed to be low awareness in most resin companies, but in the polymer companies there tended to be a high amount of awareness, but a lot of them were unable to comment. That's why I searched patents. If they had a patent dealing with nanocomposites and any polymer, I wanted to talk to them." She came across a product announcement by Imperial Chemicals about a clay emulsion on film for packaging. Japanese competitors like Showa Denko had patents on clay-polymer hybrids used for fabricating auto parts, Sumitomo had some on packaging foods, and Kuraray had filed papers to protect its R&D on plastic cooking trays, but none of them seemed to be interested in the soft drink industry.

Now the fun part, Lightfoot thought: Contacting potential customers. The first stop was the automobile industry. She asked herself, Who would care about a new material that could one day become the industry's key ingredient? This sent her scurrying back into Internet databases, where she retrieved an article in a trade publication about the trends in plastic usage and demands in making cars. The reporter had interviewed executives and engineers at Chrysler, Ford, GM, and Nissan, asking them what they thought of the demand and needs of plastics for seats and instrument panels. Lightfoot phoned every person in the article, telling them she had seen them quoted in the trade publication. To her surprise, some of them didn't even know their interviews had been published, since they had been set up by their companies' PR departments. "I can't tell you how many times I faxed them the story with their quotes in it," she says. "But this was actually helpful. By giving a little I was able to get a little." Almost to a man, the auto executives told her that if a company could provide them with a one-material car plastic that would replace the myriad polymers that make up a simple dashboard, and that would also be easily recyclable, they would line up outside the company's doors, assuming it was available at a reasonable price.

Meanwhile, Dr. Ancker was busy on his end trying to find out who had supplied Toyota with the composite it had used to produce its auto timing belt cover prototype. Ancker was a member of the Association of Consulting Chemists and Chemical Engineers and regularly attended meetings to give presentations—and schmooze. A man who held several patents and had taken to heart the advice, "Plastics, my boy, plastics," proffered in the movie *The Graduate*, he started dialing chemical industry contacts. He would ask, Who was working with Toyota on producing a more durable and heat-resistant plastic, and specifically who supplied the plastic for the experiment carried out by Akane Okada and Arimitsu

Usuki of the Toyota Central Research and Development Labs? He didn't phone Okada or Usuki directly, since he didn't know them personally; that would have to be a last resort. But it wouldn't be necessary, since Ancker's name carried a lot of weight in this world. "If I call someone, odds are he knows my name from my work, so it isn't like cold-calling," he says. "It makes it easier for me to find out information than for other people." After a month of asking around at Japanese companies and universities, Ancker discovered a company called Ube Industries that had created the polymer for Toyota. He pried open a phone book and found an Ube America in New York City. "I talked to them and they sent me some public information on a nano-size clay nylon composite, which was exactly the technology that was used in the Toyota experiment," he says. "I gave that information to Teltech."

Armed with specs on the Toyota plastic, Lightfoot, happy with the way the project was going, moved on to the beverage industry. The next stop on her informational lollapalooza was the Coca-Cola Company, which expressed a keen interest in a small, plastic bottle that would keep its products fizzy. Pepsi exhibited less interest, admitting it was aware of nano technology but wouldn't say whether it had any programs in place. Lightfoot also discovered a great deal of interest on the part of food-packaging companies, because the new plastic could withstand higher temperatures, therefore food could be packaged at a higher temperature (which is safer) and could be reheated in a microwave right in the package. Chili in a flash-frozen, heat-and-serve bucket, anyone? "Some users," Lightfoot says, "wouldn't talk to me; others were so enthusiastic they wanted to talk to my client immediately," so she passed their names on to Dow. The only companies that rejected the notion of a plastic container that offered higher performance were beer makers Coors and Miller. Both Coors and Miller were aware of the technology and had looked at the feasibility of using plastic, but the industry trend was toward glass. Plastic didn't appeal to their key demographic: twenty-five- to thirty-five-year-old males, who expressed a preference for long-neck glass bottles or cans.

Dow took the information Lightfoot had collected and used it to land a $16 million federal matching grant aimed at helping American industry be more competitive. "We spend a dollar and get a dollar back," explains Dr. Dowd. A bargain, since Dow, which earns more than $1 billion a year, paid Teltech all of $30,000 for the work. The chemical concern combined forces with a major Detroit-based auto parts supplier, Magna, and in an application to the U.S. Commerce Department claimed the plastic Dow had in the R&D phase was vital to U.S. interests. Most important, the United States was behind the Japanese (Toyota) in the race to being the first to market. They requested assistance with a basic scientific problem: How to stop the plastic from clumping when clay molecules were combined with the polymer. "For it to work, the clay has to be uniformly distributed over the polymer," Dowd says. "It's very fundamental science. Toyota had a big program in place and was ahead of us."

Not anymore. Three years after Dow applied for the grant, clay-polymer nanocomposites have still not made it to market in a meaningful way, although they are being touted for their potential. Nanocor has been notably busy, working with Eastman Chemical in approaching several container manufacturers to determine the commercial viability of its technology, and Eastman created a recycling method. It has also struck deals with AlliedSignal and Bayer.

Miller Beer, along with European brewers Carlsbad and Heineken, has introduced a plastic bottle that has solved some of the inherent problems with CO_2 leakage. The technology is not based on nanocomposites; it is a unique multilayered plastic design with a special barrier that keeps the beer as cold and fresh as in glass or aluminum. Anheuser-Busch, the nation's number one brewer, test-marketed plastic beer bottles and did indeed discover that beer drinkers were cool to them. Miller and other beer brethren, however, took their marketing tests one step further and found that fans of the amber nectar changed their opinions when they actually got to hold a bottle in their hand and taste the product. The companies don't expect plastic to replace glass or aluminum containers, on which they spend some $3.5 billion annually, but it will enable them to sell beer in places such as sports arenas, music halls, or the beach, where glass or cans may not be allowed. But there are still significant glitches. The bottles cost fifteen cents per bottle, twice as much as glass, and the smallest size available is sixteen ounces. Unlike bottles made with nanocomposites, the PET beer bottles present recycling migraines; they have a special chemical coating to keep oxygen out and CO_2 in, which means they can't be thrown in with the ubiquitous PET soda bottle for recycling.

Where is Dow? "The R&D continues to be positive," says Dr. Dowd, tight-lipped. But there is no product yet. Nevertheless, Dow, he predicts, will eventually grab 20 percent of the nanocomposite market, although it could take years. "It takes a while to change people's buying habits," he says.

As for Lightfoot, she quit Teltech in 1999 to work in curriculum development for a Minneapolis startup catering to companies that wish to improve the credentials of their corporate information technology staff. Although a "self-professed cube dweller" who cares little about the trappings of success (read: an office), Lightfoot was tired of being passed up for promotions. "Teltech is a very patriarchal place," she says.

8

Double-Cross

In Room 391 of the Thomas D. Lambrose Federal Building and Courthouse in downtown Youngstown, Ohio, Pin Yen Yang and his daughter Sally realized how alone they were.

The Yangs, the first to appear in U.S. district court to stand trial for violating the Economic Espionage Act in April 1999, weren't the only ones killing time inside the Honorable Peter C. Economus's courtroom, waiting for jury selection to begin.

They were flanked by their attorneys: Nancy Luque and Eric Dubelier from the inside-the-beltway firm of Reed Smith Shaw & McClay were charged with P. Y.'s defense, and local Cleveland defender Ralph Cascarilla remained Sally's voice in court. To their right, across the rusty-brown carpeting, was the prosecution—Marc Zwillinger, his supervisor, David E. Green, and Rodolfo Orjales, the government lawyer entrusted to handle the state's key witness: Victor Lee. Running the show was Judge Peter C. Economus, an affable, middle-aged jurist teetering on senior citizenhood.

The Yangs had ordered family and friends to steer clear of the trial, since the government would not guarantee it would not arrest others in relation to this case. "There were other people in the company involved," Zwillinger says. "We told them P. Y.'s wife was okay; we wouldn't charge her if she came, and his other daughter could also enter the U.S. without the fear of arrest. But we wouldn't make the same assurances for other members of the corporation, including Sally's husband." At least while the trial was in progress they wouldn't have to wear those clunky ankle bracelets used to monitor their movements.

The courthouse in Youngstown doesn't radiate the ambience of a grand, expansive federal building constructed out of marble and a dream. Nor does it possess the architectural aura of a building that has outlived its years. It is cleanly designed, suburban in outlook and inspiration, with white stone floors flecked with black and shined to a gleam, with glass, chrome, and rich, dark wood edited into the mix. To get to Economus's court, the Yangs had to pass through a metal detector at the front entrance, take the elevators to three, and pass through the double doors into his court, which Avery Dennison had packed with its own kind—a team of publicists, spin doctors, lawyers, and executives, "the peanut gallery" as Luque would derisively call them.

The walls were paneled in the same wood as the doors. There were no windows, no sunlight. Framing the judge were two American flags; behind him on the wall was a two-foot-high round, brass-colored seal of the United States. Put it all together and the Yangs, the only Asians (and the only accused spies) in the room, knew they were deep in enemy territory.

Along with the ideal name for a judge charged with the nation's first economic espionage case, Peter Economus, rising above the room in a high-backed black leather chair, had the right temperament. He not only had a deep understanding of the law, indeed, a passion for it mixed with a heavy dose of common sense, he had a way with people. During the course of the trial, he relied on dry wit and homespun humor to kill boredom, defuse tensions, and connect with the jurors. Although he was the sole judge working out of a one-room courthouse, he commanded attention from the feisty legal players assembled before him.

As the day wore on and prospective jurors were questioned, Yang scribbled notes, often sharing them with Luque, whereas Sally sat stoically. Months before in a phone conversation tapped by the FBI she had told Victor Lee, her friend, now ex-friend, that America was the greatest country in the world. She didn't feel that way now.

Luque and Dubelier had encountered numerous legal obstacles after meeting the captive Yang in Cleveland and taking his case. It had been seven months since Lee had officially pleaded guilty to one count of wire fraud, confessing he had stolen trade secrets for Four Pillars and agreeing to testify, to flip, for the prosecution. In the meantime, the prosecution and Avery were battling the defense over access to the material Lee had allegedly stolen on behalf of Four Pillars.

Since this was a case heavy on science, the defense had to retain experts who could explain the evidence and issues corresponding to them, and perhaps testify at trial, if the Yangs opted to mount a defense at trial. But before they could hire these experts, they needed to review the evidence—the materials used in the sting operations and formulas and letters that had allegedly changed hands. The government, however, would not hand over discovery until the three sides could hammer out an agreement that would ensure that the defense would not hire consultants or experts who had worked for an Avery competitor. This was done at Avery's behest, to protect its intellectual property, the company claimed. But Avery is such a big player in the world of glue that almost everyone the defense approached had once worked for Avery or was presently employed by or had worked for an Avery competitor. In the end, the defense would fail to locate an adhesives scientist that Avery would find acceptable.

But the big strategic move by the defense pretrial was to turn the tables on Avery in another venue in another part of world. A few months before the trial, Four Pillars announced a $262 million lawsuit filed against Avery Dennison in courts in Taiwan and China. As *Akron Beacon Journal* reporter Melanie Payne put it in the lead of her January 6, 1999, story, "The war of lawsuits and criminal cases between Avery Dennison Corp. and its Taiwanese competitor, Four Pillars Enterprise Co. Ltd., has moved from Cleveland to China."

In the suit, Four Pillars accused the American adhesives maker of fraud, claiming Avery had used information gleaned from their joint venture talks to break through barriers to the market in China and establish its own factory in Kuen Shan, China, in 1994. As a result, Four Pillars was seeking administrative relief against Avery Dennison for obtaining business secrets by fraudulent means and engaging in unfair competition.

According to Luque, "The two companies discussed a possible joint venture from 1987 to 1994." She added that during the negotiations, Avery Dennison photographed Four Pillars' proprietary machinery and used the information to open its own adhesives factory in China: "I think the issue is entry to Asia, which is a daunting task for any company," she says. "I think [Four Pillars] got blindsided by an American company."

Predictably, Avery took umbrage. "The lawsuit can best be characterized as a blatant attempt to distract attention from Four Pillars' own criminal conduct," spin-doctored Steven Fink, a company flack. He called Four Pillars' claims "completely without merit. . . . The notion that Avery Dennison would be involved in joint venture discussions with Four Pillars or any company for a period of seven years is incredible." Such discussions, he claimed, take months, not years. Fink did admit Avery had built a self-adhesive manufacturing plant in China in 1995 and has continued to expend vast resources into setting up sales offices in other Chinese cities. But these operations, he argued, are wholly unrelated to Four Pillars' claims.

While the two tape makers duked it out on a new continent, Zwillinger worked on drafting a plea bargain that would be acceptable to the defense yet include conditions that would ensure that foreign competitors would think twice before targeting another American company. The Yangs, in his mind, had already about-faced on an agreement; he had been so sure they had a deal in September that he ordered his office to cancel a court hearing.

"We assumed it would be solved by plea," Zwillinger says. "They said their clients never understood the deal, or the implication it would have for the civil trial, and when they explained it to them they didn't want to do it." Luque places the blame for the miscommunication firmly on the shoulders of P. Y. Yang's previous attorney.

They never accepted a plea, their lawyer accepted it, Luque says. "We received several offers from the prosecution and had to explain each one. It was clear no one had explained it to them beforehand. They had no concept of what a plea meant."

As a member of the Computer Crime and Intellectual Property Section of the Department of Justice, headquartered blocks away from the real DOJ in Washington, D.C., Zwillinger wanted to get this case over with as quickly as possible. With the number of computer hacker attacks on the rise, Zwillinger and his colleagues were charged with the responsibility of building cases against dozens, if not hundreds, of cybergraffiti artists and felons. In the months leading up to the Avery–Four Pillars trial, Zwillinger assisted in investigations of the Israeli hacker Ehud Tenebaum, better known as "Analyzer," who was picked up by Israeli authorities at the behest of the Department of Justice for breaching the U.S. military's computer systems. His division also opened up investigations into the well-publicized hack of the *New York Times* web site by a gang called Hacking for Girliez (HFG), which forced the *Times* to shut down its web site for nine hours after the hackers replaced *Times* content with a page of their own design; the electronic penetration of a TV satellite in California; and the swiping of declassified military software over the Internet from a military computer network. Most recently, Zwillinger was in on the investigation of the Denial of Service computer attacks in February 2000, when mammoth e-commerce sites, like Amazon, eBay, CNN, and Yahoo, were slowed to a standstill by mischievous computer pranksters. Two months after the first wave, the FBI announced an arrest in the CNN attack, which was a copycat hack. Almost every day, another computer hacker investigation crosses his desk.

Up to his starched collar in cases, Zwillinger continually rejiggered conditions in the Yangs' plea and sent them to the defense team. But one condition Zwillinger refused to yield on: P. Y. would have to serve prison time. He and his boss, Green, agreed that if P. Y. Yang didn't go to jail, this kind of conduct would be regarded as a legitimate cost of doing business.

Luque may have been even busier than Zwillinger, hopping from one case to another, arguing in person with independent prosecutor Ken Starr in Washington, D.C., one day, attending hearings for P. Y. Yang in Youngstown another day, flying to Virginia—"the rocket docket," she calls it—for still another. But as overwhelmed as she was by the sheer number of high-profile cases going to trial all at once, Luque refused to even discuss an arrangement that included Yang serving time.

The more Luque and Zwillinger went back and forth on the plea, the more intransigent they became in their positions, the more heated their conversations became, and the more they began to genuinely dislike each other. This would result in obscenity-laced blowups between the two attorneys in and out of court over the next few weeks.

Before jury selection for the April 1999 trial the judge entertained several key motions. In the first place, the defense contended, the sting should have never taken place, since Lee never did anything with the East Asian plan he had been caught peeking at. (Lee claimed he had read it but never made photocopies, nor had he passed its contents to Yang.)

In addition, the defense accused the government of relying on tainted evidence for the sting operation against Yang in Cleveland—the Avery patent on a substance Yang believed he might own; the fake Asian plan listing Four Pillars, in bold print, as an employee poaching target that had come on the heels of his battle with Avery over the young scientist Jean Guo. The material would be irresistible to Yang; it would almost assuredly be, since it had been designed to be that way by Avery Dennison. The defense purported the Yangs had been entrapped.

The defense also questioned the government's handling of the evidence, since the chain of custody had clearly been broken. It had taken Lee more than a week to turn over all of his records to Bartholomew, and two weeks for Lee to get around to handing over the "CONFIDENTIAL" scraps of paper Yang had cut with his pocketknife at the Westlake hotel. He had kept them in the bag he always carried. Never did a Bureau agent bother to search Lee's home. If the FBI had, they would have found out earlier that Lee had doctored evidence in a futile stab at protecting Yang.

More disturbing to the defense was that Avery had given Lee, the government's star witness, a reason to lie. If he hadn't, Avery could have named him in a multimillion-dollar suit against Four Pillars and the government could have put him in jail. "So we tried a pretrial motion saying they bribed him, because he is not allowed to raise evidence that Avery would find objectionable. How could he testify honestly then?" Luque asked.

Although Judge Economus didn't accede fully to the defense's wishes, he struck a unique compromise. Not sure himself of the integrity of Lee's testimony given the circumstances, he allowed the defense access to him before the trial. On the stand, if he changed his testimony from his deposition, the defense would be able to hammer him. This would also be an immense aid (and time saver) in preparing their case. "The judge let us take a deposition of the government key witness, which is unheard-of," Luque says.

But Economus also awarded the prosecution a number of significant early victories. In an attempt to keep the scope of the trial within manageable boundaries, he barred the defense from raising the issue of the joint venture, a key part of their strategy. Complains Luque: "I couldn't believe I couldn't talk about relevant and exculpatory information. Working without the joint venture material was like showing someone only the latest incident in a long-running feud."

He also ruled on several motions relating to the translations of court material–transcripts of the sting operation and letters from Lee to Four Pillars–and warned that words like "spy" and "espionage" could not be used during the trial.

But just because the people in the jury pool would not hear these dirty words in Economus's courtroom, that wouldn't prevent them from reading them on the front page of a local Youngstown newspaper, which several had. As a result, they were excluded from serving on the jury. Others departed for personal reasons. The pool shrank more when the prosecution asked potential jurors about their ability to be fair and objective in judging Asians.

There are times a defense attorney wins or loses a case before uttering a word to the jury. The not guilty verdict in the O. J. Simpson trial owes more to a change in venue from a white, law-

and-order neighborhood to the City of L.A. than it did to any fancy lawyering on the part of Simpson's attorneys. It works both ways.

The Yangs' attorneys faced a jury pool that was close to the prosecution's ideal, predominately blue collar, white, and conservative. "Since we had a minority client, we wanted minority jurors," Luque says. But there were precious few to choose from in the pool. The jury ended up with five men (three blacks) and seven women (one black). Names like Williams, Buydos, and McFarland; Dunlap and Phillip; Maigetter, Semko, Hartill, and Brakus; Mason, Lucas, and Combs. These twelve faceless men and women, none of whom had ever laid their eyes on P. Y. Yang before, would be the ones to decide his fate.

The state's case against Four Pillars rested primarily on two things: Victor Lee and the videotape of the hotel sting. Prosecutors had a signed confession from one of the defendants, Victor Lee, who implicated his coconspirators. He had kept meticulous records and with his help the government had been able to reconstruct a chain of events that, in their minds, constituted economic espionage. They also had in their hands a videotape, and juries, they knew, like to be shown a crime, not just hear evidence of one. If a picture is worth a thousand words, what is a video worth? Perhaps the difference between freedom and incarceration.

But their video didn't just show Yang in the act of cutting away the words "CONFIDENTIAL" and "For Internal Eyes Only," a clear violation of the EEA as interpreted by the Third Circuit Court of Appeals—the intent to steal trade secrets. The tape also included a damning conversation. P. Y. Yang reminds Lee to be discreet, after what had occurred in the Taxol case, indicating he knew what he was doing was wrong. Yang punctuated his legal troubles with this final command to Lee: "You can collect or get some new samples, or the new research trends. Whatever tomorrow's product, we have to develop it earlier. . . . We do not need to copy the thing. We can modify it."

It was the ideal prosecutorial dirt: perpetrators snagged on camera, betrayed by their own words and actions, their intent made clear to those who would decide their guilt. "The evidence in the case is overwhelming," said Avery executive Lee Caldwell. "For Pete's sake, Dr. Lee signed a confession."

But where the government saw a slam dunk victory, the defense saw sloppy prosecutorial conduct, a case riddled with holes. And Dubelier and Luque, both of whom had worked as prosecutors, knew how to exploit weaknesses in the government's case. The feds had blown the investigation. There had been no chain of custody with the evidence. Lee had taken two weeks to turn over all his records to agent Bartholomew, and an additional two weeks to give him the scraps of "CONFIDENTIAL" clippings from the hotel sting. Luque and Dubelier were beginning to think that FBI stood for Federal Bureau of Incompetence.

They knew they would be able to impeach Lee. Luque would hinge much of her opening argument on the notion that Victor Lee was a liar who had trumped up charges against the Yangs in exchange for a bribe—diminished punishment. Perhaps the most potent point on the defense's side was that most of Lee's activities covered in the plethora of mail and wire fraud charges had taken place before the passage of the Economic Espionage Act and were also beyond the legal statute of limitations: seven years.

Dubelier says he thought it "particularly preposterous" that the prosecution would charge the Yangs with money laundering, a charge intended to be levied against organized crime and drug dealers. The government claimed that Yang paying Lee through his sister-in-law constituted money laundering. If anyone was guilty of money laundering, it would have been Lee. The government was just piling up charges. It would be laughable if it weren't so serious. The money-laundering charge alone carried a sentence of up to twenty years. As for the two charges under the EEA, the defense contended the act was designed to prevent high-tech, defense-oriented secrets from falling into the hands of foreign governments, not to assist a company competing for an advantage in the glue market.

Luque and Dubelier thought they could get the bulk of the counts dismissed before trial's end. The judge had already appeared to be sympathetic to their plight of battling a corporation in a corporate town. He had given the defense access to Lee in a deposition. He had struck potential jurors who he feared might have been tainted by a newspaper article, something many law-and-order judges wouldn't do. He had ordered Avery to remove an American flag from a video the company had created to show how a label is created.

He was clearly willing, even eager, to be creative under the right circumstances. If it weren't for the video the government probably wouldn't have bothered to prosecute the case. Although Zwillinger refuses to speculate, he admits that if the Yangs hadn't been caught on camera, it would have been a non–Economic Espionage Act case.

The time of the Yangs' trial, spring 1999, was a heady time for America. The new tech economy was humming along, new records were established almost daily on the NASDAQ. The number of North Americans plugged into cyberspace was approaching 100 million. Crime was down, unemployment so low in some places that fry cooks in fast-food restaurants in certain midwestern cities were earning $10 an hour and signing up for 401(K) plans. IPO fever was in full outbreak, producing instant billionaires (on paper at least), and America's biggest headache was the war in a place that was once Yugoslavia. And the post office celebrated the production of the first 427 million new Daffy Duck self-adhesive postage stamps by Avery Dennison.

Prior to giving his opening statement, Zwillinger had worked two consecutive seventy-hour workweeks with his colleagues, prepping for his first Department of Justice trial. At this point he knew as much about adhesives as some scientists. He could tell you the difference between a polymer physicist, a rheologist, and your run-of-the-mill glue sniffer. He knew it could take twenty layers of chemicals to produce just one adhesive, and that Avery had created more than 200 types of adhesives in its vaults. He knew the definitions of "master curve" and "tackifier." On April 1, 1999, two years after starting work at the Department of Justice, Zwillinger stood to face the jury for his opening statement.

"This is a case about stealing," he said, scanning their eyes. He had once lost election for class president in eleventh grade (so the pragmatic Zwillinger became class secretary instead) and was determined to not repeat the defeat here. He began by offering the jury the gist of the state's case against the Yangs: Victor Lee, a scientist at adhesives maker Avery Dennison, had spent seven years passing some of the company's dearest technological secrets to a Taiwanese competitor, Four Pillars.

Zwillinger told the jury about Lee and Avery Dennison and how Lee had come to meet Yang in Taiwan. "Pleased that he had information that was valuable to the chairman of Four Pillars and enthusiastic about helping a Taiwanese company develop a label business, Dr. Lee took the deal."

Zwillinger mapped out the prosecution's case and the jurors listened attentively. There is an advantage to going first. At the start of a trial there is a kinetic energy in the air, the sense that something of great value is up for grabs, in this case, the Yangs' freedom. Fresh-scrubbed, shaved, and caffeinated, jurors tend to be more alert. They would become more bleary-eyed as the trial dragged on and they were force-fed massive doses of adhesives jargon, labels lingo, and the life and times of Victor Lee.

For now, however, here was the dashing Zwillinger, who promised jurors he would produce evidence that would show the

Yangs knowingly received valuable reports and other information from Lee in exchange for $160,000. He also said he would prove the Yangs schemed to defraud Avery Dennison not only of confidential and proprietary information, but also of "the honest services of Dr. Lee," whom Zwillinger admitted the jury might find "defensive," "stubborn," "disloyal," and "pathetic." "As you listen to [Lee] tell you that he was flattered by all the attention he received from the defendants and in Taiwan, that he was proud to be considered an important man back in his country, and that he was proud to be making extra money for his family, you may or may not like him," Zwillinger said. He also drew attention to a videotape showing that the Yangs "conspired to take and attempted to take a trade secret belonging to Avery Dennison" relating to a patent application.

> As you watch the videotape on the big screen that will come down behind me, and see [Victor Lee] provide these confidential materials, you will watch as the defendant P. Y. Yang reaches into his pocket and takes out a pocketknife, and you will see that he folds the documents Dr. Lee gives him slowly and carefully and then he uses his pocketknife to cut out any portion of the documents that's marked "Avery Dennison" or that lists the names of Avery Dennison employees. And you will watch as he gives these cuttings to Dr. Lee and tells him not once, not twice, but three times not to throw these cuttings out in the hotel trash, but to take them home and throw them out [there]. But Dr. Lee didn't throw them out at home. He gave them to the FBI.

Zwillinger also promised the video would show P. Y. Yang asking his daughter Sally to cut out parts of the sting material. "You will see them on the videotape sitting there side by side cutting and taping the documents so that they would stay together with the parts removed, cutting and taping until all the evidence that these documents had come from Avery Dennison was removed. Then you will see that they put the documents in their luggage and took them with them."

He paused, then did what every good prosecutor does. He told the jury what he expected of them. You can't ask twelve strangers to send a man and woman to prison unless you can look them right in the eye and say, "When you have seen the videotapes, heard from Dr. Lee, read through the documents, and seen all the evidence in this case, we will return and stand before you and we will ask you to return verdicts of guilty against both individual defendants, P. Y. Yang and Sally Yang, and the company they worked for and ran, Four Pillars, on all the charges brought against them in this case."

Nancy Luque had watched Zwillinger's performance from the defense bench with disdain. After some instant pleasantries, she said:

> Ladies and gentlemen, I am here to tell you that the evidence will show that in this case, the case you just heard Mr. Zwillinger talk about, the same case you are about to hear me talk about, is based entirely, *entirely*, on the evidence that you will hear from one witness. That witness is Victor Lee. Marc Zwillinger isn't a witness, he doesn't know as he stood here today whether what he was telling you was true. He wasn't there, he didn't see it, he didn't know about it when it was happening. He has to rely on Victor Lee.

She had drafted her speech with Lee as her linchpin later. First she had to assault his character. By the time she was done, she wanted each juror to analyze every word the government's star snitch said and, equally important, the way he said it. Luque wanted them to peer into Lee's eyes, to search for nervous tics, fidgety fingers, a change in facial pallor. She wanted them to assume Lee would lie. That would make it all the more sweet later in the trial when her cocounsel in crime, Dubelier, got to flip that flipper on the stand. Luque asked the jury to consider some important questions when it came to Lee. Did he have any reason to lie? Were there any other pieces of evidence from a source other than Lee that could corroborate his claims?

Before she moved on she attacked Lee's credibility one last time, in case she hadn't hammered home the point enough.

I heard Mr. Zwillinger already apologize for Victor Lee, already telling you, you may not believe him. You may find him sympathetic, you may not. The other thing I think I heard Mr. Zwillinger say is Victor Lee has already lied to Avery on many occasions. Well, if Victor Lee lied to Avery, then how can we believe that he's telling Mr. Zwillinger the truth, that he's telling you the truth? The evidence is going to show that Victor Lee has many, many reasons to lie. The evidence is going to show that there is no independent evidence, and Mr. Zwillinger has already said he's been dishonest.

Luque transitioned into her second point: books. Victor Lee was a consultant who spoke the same language as the Yangs, not just Mandarin and Taiwanese, but the language of glue. Four Pillars was impressed enough with Lee to hire him to provide "information, public information. Information that is very difficult to get, at least in 1989, in Taiwan," Luque said. "No Amazon.com, no information superhighway. The books aren't in the libraries as they are in this country." Lee had been hired to teach because it was cheaper for Four Pillars to hire Lee than to send someone to the United States to collect textbooks, some Lee had used in graduate school, magazines, research papers, and other "public scientific information," she said. It was a thin argument, but she knew it would be flushed out later on Dubelier's cross-examination of Lee, when the defense planned to dump a mound of material on the evidence table in front of the jury—some five dozen books Lee had mailed off to Taiwan for which Four Pillars had reimbursed him, textbooks on topics like polymer science and rheology. "There is absolutely no reason to believe that that relationship was anything other than a relationship that any company would have with any outside consultant," Luque continued. "Curiously, Mr. Zwillinger didn't tell you about a whole other relationship. Victor Lee had a relationship with Four Pillars, but so did Avery. . . . "

Zwillinger shifted uneasily in his seat. Had he heard her right? Was Luque trying to sneak the joint venture into her opening argument? This was clearly off limits. The judge had been explicit. But Zwillinger didn't want to lodge an objection. There is an unwritten rule: Neither side objects during an opening statement, since it disrupts the flow. With both sides mutually vulnerable, it was a courtesy that had withstood the test of time.

"During the course of the Victor Lee–Four Pillars relationship Avery and Four Pillars had a relationship," Luque continued. "In fact it started before the Victor Lee relationship. It was a discussion about going into business together in China."

Zwillinger couldn't believe his ears. "Objection!" he shouted.

This first contentious encounter set the tone for the rest of the trial.

By the time Victor Lee was put on the witness stand everyone in Judge Economus's Youngstown courtroom—jurors, attorneys, judge, bailiffs, court reporters, clerks, spectators, journalists, Avery publicists—was sick of the seven-word query, "Your Honor, may we approach the bench?" It got so bad that at one point in the trial, after defense attorney Dubelier asked for yet another sidebar conference, Judge Economus replied, "Are you trying to get even with me now?"

The judge said he was kidding. But attorneys from both sides were also struck by the unusually high number of hostile sidebars. A week into the trial and already there were the inevitable bitter jokes that it might never end. The defense contested every piece of evidence. The prosecutors charged the defense with purposely mischaracterizing its motives. And the judge navigated the daily squalls with a calm, steady hand, except for the occasional outburst when he felt things getting out of hand. He gave both sides wide latitude to raise points of law and discuss how to lay proper legal foundations for each piece of evidence. And there was a mound of evidence. This slowed the proceedings to a crawl. Rodolfo Orjales, who was handling the government's direct questioning of Lee, believed the disruptions were "driving [the jury] nuts."

When the government introduced the videotape for Lee to narrate for the jury, Orjales managed to get through just one question before Dubelier objected and asked to approach the bench. The defense had tried everything they could think of to exclude Lee and the videotape from the trial. In several motions they argued the FBI sting used to trap the Yangs should have never taken place because Lee had never sent to Yang the restricted Avery document he had been caught looking at. The defense claimed the FBI had entrapped the Yangs. It tried to have all of Lee's testimony excluded, claiming he had been pressured and manipulated by a vengeful Avery and the FBI.

If Lee testified against Avery in any way, the company could suspend the agreement with him and soak him for millions in its civil action against Four Pillars. The contract included a clause that mandated that Lee

cooperate fully with AVERY DENNISON in the investigation of the facts, circumstances, extent and effects of the misappropriation of AVERY DENNISON's confidential information and trade secrets. Such cooperation shall include, but not be limited to . . . the full, candid and truthful disclosure of all facts known to him relating to such misappropriation; providing to AVERY DENNISON all documentary and other evidence relating to such misappropriation; providing full, candid and truthful testimony about such misappropriation in any proceeding, civil or criminal and wherever venued, arising from or relating thereto.

The defense contended that Lee read the agreement in a way that required him to tell the truth as long as it worked to Avery Dennison's benefit.

Dubelier wanted to make it difficult for the prosecution to get the video in via Lee's testimony. "This whole thing is a setup," he said. "For Victor Lee to explain what he was referring to he'd have to preface every answer [with] 'I was reading lines I was fed by the FBI because it was all a setup to begin with.'" He objected to Victor Lee going back after the fact and providing his own interpretations of the tape, when the tape should speak for itself. It didn't matter what Lee meant to say or think or do; all that mattered was what he had done and said on the tape.

"I haven't even asked him a question yet," protested Orjales in a rare sidebar appearance. Well, he was the one in the middle of this latest storm.

"He's not filling in the blanks, he's just testifying," the judge said. "The tape is a separate piece of evidence. He's also testifying. He can testify to what took place."

"This tape shouldn't be admitted," reasoned Cascarilla.

"If [Lee] is explaining something he said, that's not testifying what took place," Dubelier said.

"I don't think he's explaining, he's just expressing," Economus said. "Go ahead, I'm going to let it in."

While Zwillinger ran the video player, fast-forwarding to precise numbered points, Orjales used Lee to bury the Yangs. This was a crucial moment in the trial. The video was the next best thing to being an eyewitness. Jurors got to see what actually happened. They could see body language for themselves. They could see how Lee interacted with the Yangs. They could see the crime being committed. They would see that the Yangs knew what they were doing was wrong and draw their own conclusions. The prosecution planned on getting a lot of mileage out of the sting. Zwillinger stopped the video at 13:50:30.

"What was the document you handed to P. Y. [Yang] at this portion of the video?" Orjales asked Lee, a forgotten man in all the hubbub.

"It was a patent pending [FBI Special Agent] Mike Bartholomew gave me on the same morning," Lee said.

"And who was the applicant on that patent application?"

"You mean the author?"

"Yes," Orjales said. "The company filing the patent."

"I think that belonged to Avery," Lee said.

Zwillinger inched the video forward, then stopped. Eyes not on the videotaped images of Sally and P. Y. Yang on the screen were on the faces of the real Sally and P. Y. in court.

"Dr. Lee," Orjales said, "could you tell what P. Y. was pointing to on the document being held by Sally when he said, 'Cut that out'?"

"He was pointing to the confidential sign, note, stickers," Lee said.

A few more questions and Judge Economus shut down the proceedings for the day. The following Monday Orjales and Zwillinger kept the pressure on.

"Are Government's Exhibits 75, 76, 77, and 78 true and correct copies of the documents in the form that you provided to the defendants on September 4, 1997?" Orjales asked Lee.

"Yes," Lee said, recognizing the patent and Asian expansion plan that had been used as sting bait.

"Focusing, if you would, Dr. Lee, on Government's Exhibit 75, were the headings here in this kind of format when you provided them to the defendants, this distribution list, for example?"

"Yes."

"Looking at Government's 76, were the Avery logo and the confidential sticker on Government's 76 when you handed it to the defendants in September of 1997?"

"Yes."

"How about this heading here, 'CONFIDENTIAL.' Was that there?"

"Yes." Zwillinger reversed the tape two minutes back. When Luque saw what was on the screen, she tried not to catch Dubelier's eye, but it was hard.

"Dr. Lee," Orjales said, "from where you were seated in the room on September 4th, 1997, could you see what, if anything, P. Y. Yang was holding in his hand at this moment?"

"It was a pocketknife," Lee said.

"Dr. Lee. . . . Could you see what Sally Yang was doing to these documents?"

"Your Honor, objection," Dubelier cut in. "Form of the question."

"Overruled."

"Sally was cutting a portion of the paper out of the document on P. Y.'s request." Tape played. Tape stopped. Damning image, damning question, damning answer. Tape played. Tape stopped. Another damning image, another damning question, another damning answer. Dubelier pretended it didn't bother him. Luque offered silent succor to her client. Cascarilla copped calm. The Yangs studied the air in front of them, as Orjales, Lee, and Zwillinger continued to taunt them with the evidence.

Who told you to take the cuttings? Orjales asked.

"P. Y.," Lee said.

The way he said it almost sounded like "case closed."

Not all of the trial was filled with such *High Noon* drama, although it had its moments for both sides.

Most notably, an interesting change in Lee emerged as Dubelier began to cross-exam the disgraced polymer physicist. Instead of stonewalling, Dubelier and Luque got the distinct impression Lee was trying to help the Yangs. As a result, they changed strategy midstream, from trying to obliterate Lee's character and raising doubt about the truthfulness of his testimony, to treating him as a friendly witness, coaxing from him information that was damaging to the government's case.

Dubelier started his cross by entering some sixty books into evidence, Lee patiently identifying each and every one. He was almost eager to admit they were available at most college bookstores.

Lee also informed the court that Yang had never specifically asked him for Avery trade secrets, and that no one from the FBI had ever searched his home for other potentially pertinent documents; instead he had taken two weeks to transfer his records to Agent Bartholomew at Avery Fasson Roll headquarters. As a result, there had been no chain of custody for the evidence, indicating sloppy investigative work on the part of the feds. The defense would argue that the prosecution could not then guarantee the integrity of the evidence. How did they know that any material Lee turned over to the feds had been received by the Yangs, and in the same condition?

More injurious to the government's case was Lee's testimony on Jean (Jong) Guo, the young Four Pillars scientist Avery recruited in 1996. He was the one who had initially tipped Avery off to Lee's activities, the impetus for all of Avery's subsequent actions. The government claimed that Lee contacted Yang to warn him of Guo's impending hiring, afraid the former Four Pillars scientist would blow his cover.

Lee's version was substantially different. He said he had called Yang simply to inform him that Guo was applying for a job and would probably be coming to Avery for an interview. (Lee, along with everyone else in his section, had received a copy of Guo's résumé.) Yang called back in an hour, telling Lee that, according to the contract he had signed with the company, Guo was barred from taking any job at Avery. That was all it took to prompt Yang to mail threatening letters to Avery. But it was clear that Yang wasn't trying to protect Lee's cover. He just wanted to stop a bitter rival from hiring an employee who knew some of Four Pillars' most valuable industrial secrets.

But it was on the second day of Dubelier's cross-examination that Lee threw the case into a tizzy. The defense had entered into evidence a letter Lee had sent the Yangs in which the confidential markings had been removed.

"And the 'CONFIDENTIAL' markings were removed by you; is that correct?" Dubelier asked Lee.

"Yes."

"When were they removed?" Dubelier asked, already sure of the answer.

"Before I sent it," Lee admitted.

Dubelier asked Lee which version of the letter he kept at home, the one later turned over to the FBI.

"The one with the confidential markings," Lee said.

Dubelier asked Lee if he had ever informed the FBI that he was the one who had removed the confidential markings from the letter.

"I was never asked," Lee said. "They never asked," Dubelier repeated. That was a startling omission, but no surprise to Dubelier, who had learned of this a week earlier when he had questioned Lee without the jury present. He knew if he played his cards right, he could cast doubt on every single piece of evidence Lee had provided from his home for this trial, which made up the evidence for eighteen of twenty-one of the counts.

"So what you're saying is, all the discussions you had during March of 1997 with Special Agent Bartholomew, he never asked you whether or not the documents you were giving him were in the same form as the ones you sent to Four Pillars?" Dubelier said.

"That's correct."

"When is the first time that was ever asked of you?"

"Sometime last week." In this courtroom.

Dubelier wanted to make sure every single juror recognized the importance of this moment. He boiled it down once more. "So what you're telling us is, from the time this case began in March of 1997, the first time anyone from the government ever asked you whether or not the documents you sent to Four Pillars were in the same form as the documents you've turned over to the FBI was Tuesday or Wednesday of last week?"

Lee was interrupted by a flurry of government objections. Dubelier was only happy to rephrase the question. Now there could be no way a juror could fail to understand what was occurring.

"Did you at any time prior to last Tuesday or Wednesday ever tell the government that there were certain documents, including Government's Exhibit 7, that were in a different condition when you sent them to Four Pillars than they were when you gave them to the FBI?"

"No, I was not asked."

In the end, the judge would dismiss eighteen of the twenty-one counts filed against the Yangs, including the most serious one, money laundering, which carried a penalty of up to twenty years in prison. He left one count of mail fraud and two counts of violating the nation's trade secrecy laws, which carried a penalty of up to ten years in jail. Then the jury returned with its verdict.

"Of the three counts, with respect to mail fraud, the jury finds the defendants, each of the defendants in this case, not guilty."

The defense shared a shallow collective sigh.

Economus continued: "With respect to the charge of conspiracy to commit theft of a trade secret, the jury finds each defendant guilty," he said. "With respect to the charge of attempted theft of a trade secret, all defendants are also found guilty."

In a later hearing, Economus sentenced P. Y. Yang to six more months in Cleveland exile, gave Sally probation, and fined Four Pillars $5 million, the maximum amount under the statute.

And with that, America's first trial under the Economic Espionage Act of 1996 came to a close.

"Avery captured the king," Luque says bitterly. "Four Pillars is a one-man company, and while P. Y. is stuck in Cleveland, Avery has been invading China."

The following January, the civil trial began, the verdict a foregone conclusion, since the guilty verdict in the criminal case was taken into account. The Yangs had a new codefendant, Victor Lee, who was being punished by Avery for having aided and abetted the defense during the trial. Avery was awarded $40 million.

Three weeks later, in late February 2000, Avery Dennison issued a press release, announcing that it will invest more than $40 million to expand its operations in China. "At a news conference in Shanghai, China, Avery Dennison senior managers said the company will build three new facilities in China over the next two years, expand its existing Kunshan manufacturing plant and open a professional training center for label printers and converters," the release said.

9

Chief Hacking Officer

Marc Maiffret, his hair purple, spiky, and coated in gel, doesn't look like an operative paid to steal what a Kashmiri terrorist believed was top-secret U.S. military software. Partial to black pants and silk button-down shirts, Maiffret likes "to dress like Nicolas Cage," but at five foot six he's built more like a neo-Gothic version of Barney Rubble.

It has come as no surprise to the twenty-year-old cybersavant known as "Chameleon" that life is a numbers game. For as long as he can remember, the digital intruder turned Internet security guru has existed in a netherworld of digits. Zeroes and ones "that I manipulated and that manipulated me," strung together in the language of binary code, are the basis of the commands he used to forge the applications that underlie the operating systems that serve as the brains of the computer networks he breaks into.

Chameleon, who specializes in tearing apart Microsoft software for security holes, says, "I didn't graduate from MIT with top honors. My world has revolved around breaking software and systems while the security professionals' world has revolved around fixing and securing their systems against me and my attacks—attacks they know nothing about."

Now, as a cofounder of eEye, a top Internet security consulting firm, he has become one of those computer security pros he used to outfox. Maiffret has business cards, but that doesn't mean he has gone mainstream. After all, they read, "Chief Hacking Officer." He, and antiestablishment propeller-heads like him, with hacker handles like "Jericho," "Dildog," "Punkis," and "Tweety Fish," personify why corporate espionage has not yet been retrofitted for cyberspace.

But how tempting it must be for corporate America. Already most companies store vast caches of valuable data—including personnel records, customer billing, confidential financial information, confidential blueprints, marketing plans, and technologies in the R&D stage—in their computer networks. From a remote location anywhere in the world, a skilled digital intruder could sneak into a corporate network by tricking the network software to run his commands and not those of the system administrator. Once inside, he could jump from machine to machine, copying documents and confidential e-mail. A world of bits and bytes, since he leaves his bounty behind as well as taking it with him, a company wouldn't even know it had been hacked—unless the perp bragged.

"I think as businesses move more data online, their competitors will find it tempting to hire hackers," says Dale Coddington, systems security engineer for eEye Digital Security. "Since the FBI's track record catching them is less than stellar, there's little chance a well-trained hacker will get caught. With such low risk and high reward, it's inevitable some company is going to get burned through cyberspace. The question is, will it even know about it?"

Since the dawn of electronic time (the 1960s) computer hackers have roamed "cyberspace"—even before that word was first coined by sci-fi writer William Gibson in the 1984 paperback *Neuromancer*. At first the Internet connected a select group of universities and research institutions; the term "hacker" was either used to describe someone with a bad golf swing or a geek who explored the innermost workings of computer systems. In neither instance was a hacker a lawbreaker. He usually attained his skills by spending thousands of hours spelunking through large networks, studying how they were cobbled together. The invention of the World Wide Web in 1989 changed all this. At first the Information Superhighway was a mere backcountry road, riddled with potholes and service disruptions. As late as 1996 most Americans had never heard of the web, the word "browser" was used to describe someone wandering around a store without a plan, and few corporations maintained a presence in cyberspace.

As the 1990s hustled forward companies began to recognize the inevitability of business-to-consumer e-commerce, and by 2000 there were millions of web sites, many of them belonging to corporations and small businesses, as well as universities, research centers, think tanks, mom-and-pop operations, religious and political zealots, porn providers, online scammers and hate groups, newspapers, magazines, and publishing houses, hackers, and music and software pirates, as well as your regular Joe and Josephine Q. Public.

But more web sites means more computer assaults. In 1988, the first year for which statistics are available, there were 6 reported hacking incidents, according to CERT (part of Carnegie Mellon University's Software Engineering Institute). Four years later there were 773. The year 1995 saw 2,412 attacks launched on computers, with the number quadrupling to 9,859 in the year 1999. The first quarter of 2000 continued this trend, setting a pace that should easily eclipse 10,000 hacks for the year. And these are just the reported ones. The Pentagon alone suffers hundreds of attacks a week, as do scores of other government and military sites. Motorola, the *New York Times,* and Yahoo! are just a few of the companies that have had their web sites taken over by obstreperous digital felons.

Greater global interconnectedness isn't just part of a cybergeek's daily musings, it has also been working its way into the mainstream. Horror flick sequels specialist Wes Craven (director of *Scream* et al. and numerous *Nightmares on Elm Street*) says: "I look at computers and their growing global linkage as the beginning of neural pathways to planet consciousness. It began with the telegraph, the foundation for using numbers to convey information, to the computers of today. The way that computers are growing closer together, linked by the Internet, creates a digital central nervous system. There's a brain forming around the skin of the planet."

Trippy, maybe. But this greater human virtual connectivity comes at a price: security. The ease with which a massive wave of "denial of service" (DOS) attacks were launched against powerhouse e-commerce success stories in February 2000 illustrates that everyone, even the richest corporation, is equally vulnerable in cyberspace. Yahoo!, E*Trade, Amazon, Buy.com, and a score of other sites were hit with a hailstorm of tiny electronic packets containing anticorporate messages. The company's routers and servers hyperventilated from the onslaught, slowing traffic to a crawl and in some cases shutting down the network. In real-world terms it was the equivalent of a million irate PC owners simultaneously dialing twenty frazzled tech-support operators. The result: a stream of busy signals and a whole lot of frustrated customers.

"Hackers have known for a long time a large-scale DOS like this could be done, but no one's had the chutzpah to do it before," says Tweety Fish, a member of "Cult of the Dead Cow," an underground hacker organization the DOS attackers sent greetings to within the code used to flood targets. (Dead Cow members had nothing to do with it.)

Computer security company ICSA estimates there are one million hackers around the globe, many of them "script kiddies," or wannabes who wouldn't know computer code from Morse code but who get behind corporate firewalls by relying on point-and-click software available from hacker sites on the Internet—free for the asking, for those who know where to surf.

But don't expect corporations to turn to hackers to find out what rivals are up to any time soon. Corporate suits don't trust computer culture kids like Maiffret and have even less desire to work with them; usually the only time corporate IT departments interface with his kind is when the company's home page has been graffitied by some script kiddie. When companies hire computer experts from the outside, it is usually for computer forensics, another hot field. This is used to catch a disgruntled employee stealing data or to nab someone distributing confidential material via e-mail. In 1998 Maiffret was hired to gather evidence for a civil suit. The client's spiteful ex-lover had stolen the license for a valuable microsurgical clamp from his company, AroSurgical of Newport Beach, California. Maiffret specially coded software to monitor her corporate e-mail account, hoping she would be reckless enough to continue using it. He was pleased when she did, dialing in from home. Maiffret didn't monitor her outgoing e-mail but he could see the incoming messages.

> Every ten minutes the program would check her e-mail account, make copies, and send them to us, a program that it took me about forty-five minutes to code. We could have used the Microsoft Outlook program, but I didn't want files removed from the server, because then she wouldn't have gotten her mail and gotten suspicious.

One of the e-mails came from a company she had solicited that mentioned the existence of the document and would they be interested in talking. AroSurgical got an injunction, barring her from using the pilfered license, and eEye got to bill $240 an hour.

Maiffret believes he has the creativity to solve almost any problem on the fly—and that's because of his hacker roots. But many
computer security firms claim they won't hire people like him.
They say they are fearful of a criminal past.

ISS, an Internet security company headquartered in Atlanta, has
for years decried the use of hackers by its competitors. The company guarantees its employees have pure pasts by conducting extensive background checks. But, points out Space Rogue, publisher
of the *Hacker News Network* and a member of the L0pht Heavy Industries, a hacker think tank in Boston, companies already hire
hackers, they just don't know it.

"There is no national hacker registry to check on someone's
hacker status," says Space Rogue, who, along with other members
of L0pht, testified before Congress in 1998 about threats to the National Electronic Infrastructure. "Any company that comes out and
claims, 'We do not hire hackers' is deluding itself," he continues.

ISS CEO Christopher Klaus, who kicked off his company in
1994 with a single product, calls hiring hackers "a questionable
practice, which could lead to tremendous legal liability." The $3
billion company, housed in Atlanta, refers to itself as "the world's
leading provider of security management solutions for the Internet," claiming more than 5,000 customers, including twenty-one of
the twenty-five largest U.S. commercial banks, nine of the ten
largest telecommunications companies, and more than thirty-five
government agencies. Klaus, himself a reformed hacker who used
the identity "Coup," would have a lot to lose if he brought in the
wrong guys.

But ISS has in fact hired a half a dozen or more known hackers
in recent years, some who have the reputation for being quite malicious, including one who goes by the name "Prym" and has been
linked to a number of high-profile assaults on corporate, government, military, and proenvironmental web sites: "Phree Kevin Mit-

nick or we will club 600 baby seals," the nasty teen once scrawled across GreenPeace's home page. (At the time hacker Kevin Mitnick was in prison, and a major cause célèbre.)

Klaus admits Prym was on ISS's payroll, but "it was mutually decided we would part company. He no longer works at ISS." Another ISS employee edited the hacker 'zine *Phrack*, and at least two others coded hacker software exploits that somehow got into the wild. These exploits, some computer professionals say, were responsible for thousands of successful computer attacks over an eighteen-month period. Although Klaus says that he knew nothing about the extracurricular hacktivities of some of the young professionals he hired for his "X-Team," a much-hyped special security unit within the company, it's been an open secret in hacking circles for years.

Hackers like Maiffret detest law enforcement, distrust government, and can't stand corporations. Even when one of their own—Coup—turned corporate, he became, in their eyes, a hypocrite by disavowing his roots. Hackers' currency is up-to-the-second information, the lifeblood of their vocations. Who'd want to help a corporation make money? Besides, those who come equipped with the highest hacker skill levels often carry on two lives: In the virtual world they are shadowy figures who explore the farthest reaches of cyberspace for security holes. They create new scripts, sometimes malicious, contact software vendors to warn them about flaws in their products, set up web sites to comment on the scene, and publish copies of hacked corporate home pages (available at www.attrition.org).

They are often computer activists with a bent for anarchy. Information, the old hacker credo goes, wants to be free. In the real world, however, that same information about hacking and security vulnerabilities reaps them six-figure salaries as network consultants. Just because they are upper-income-earning, tax-paying, law-abiding citizens when they are not wired into their computers doesn't mean they have changed their worldviews. Hacking isn't just the accumulation of a special set of skills, it's a way of life, an obsession, more a new type of millennial philosophy than a job description at an "information resource" company.

No one better personifies this than Dildog, also a member of Cult of the Dead Cow, who was lounging in his hotel suite at the 1999 Defcon hacking convention, a smile smeared on his face. It being Las Vegas in July, the temperature outside was 100 degrees, but Dildog was air-conditioned cool. The unveiling of his latest software upgrade for "Back Orifice," a not-so-subtle dig at Microsoft's Back Office, had been a rousing success. The software is a corporate spook's hottest fantasy tool. Once installed on a target's computer network (it could be secretly planted merely by sending it as an e-mail attachment) it gave the user total access and control. From a remote location, a spy could explore every nook and cranny of the system and analyze every single activity, as if he were the systems administrator. He could capture all passwords and keystrokes, copy all documents and files, hop unhindered from machine to machine, from web server to e-mail files, surf through databases containing vast caches of credit cards, and wiggle his way into vast stores of personal information gathered from customers. The software also came equipped with programs that could turn on and control built-in microphones and PC cameras without the user knowing. Anyone could be watched and recorded at any time. Call it the Corporate Cam.

But that's not why Dildog, who earns big bucks at an established technology company, created it. Although software makers, computer security companies, antivirus makers, and law enforcement claimed the release of Back Orifice 2000 was just a way for hackers to legitimize illegal computer intrusions, Dildog says he is just trying to point out potential problems with Microsoft's software.

Computer security companies are "afraid to admit that their detection system is horribly and possibly irreparably flawed," he says. "[They] give people the impression their software 'raises the bar' against the average hacker. Unfortunately, this also fools people with really critical networks into thinking that this software is sufficient to protect them. People trusting this stuff to protect them . . . are in for a surprise."

A gaggle of followers, most of them in their twenties and dressed in *noir* black, with tattoos, piercings, and scraggly hair, waited for Dildog in his hotel suite. They sat cross-legged on the carpet, availing themselves to a well-stocked minibar piled high with bottles of vodka, bourbon, and whiskey. Of the 3,000 hackers, crackers, geeks, "scene whores" (hacker groupies), computer security professionals, journalists, undercover cops, and federal agents who attended the 1999 Defcon hacker convention, 2,000 of them had crammed into a conference room at the Alexis Park Hotel to watch the BO2K release. The year before, Cult of the Dead Cow had chosen Defcon to promote the first version of its Back Orifice. Written by fellow Cult member Sir Dystic, it worked on Windows 95 and 98 machines by secretly creating a back door so that a remote user could control all functions on those computers.

The upgrade Dildog-coded version had been designed to work with networks that run on Windows NT, and it camouflaged itself extremely well. Cult of the Dead Cow members didn't travel all the way to Las Vegas to disappoint. They kicked off the conference with a laser light show, culminating in a deafening electronic moo sound. The crowd gyrated and cheered. Then, while Dildog and his associates explained their don't-blame-us-if-Microsoft-products-suck philosophy, a CD-ROM label was projected on the wall behind them, a cow head spinning and spinning. At the end of the presentation, Cult members flung two dozen CD-ROMs containing the Back Orifice update. The crowd surged forward. Antivirus makers and computer security company reps watched closely, hoping to later corral someone with a copy. The first one to crack the program would win bragging rights, their names in a press release, perhaps even a mention in some magazine or newspaper articles as heroes who thwarted the evil intentions of the Cult of the Dead Cow hacker gang.

An employee of ISS threw himself into the mob and somehow snagged a copy. Within twenty-four hours, the company would crack parts of the program and release an application that could identify it. At the time, Dildog didn't know this, and even if he had he wouldn't have cared. In an earlier Internet conversation, according to Dildog, an ISS employee had approached him and asked how much of a bribe it would take for him to pass the company an advance copy of the software, he claims. "Money doesn't motivate us," he said, but as a joke the Cult sent the ISS minion back a note saying it would take $1 million and a monster truck. Later, Cult members would be chagrined to discover the original discs dispersed at Defcon had been infected with the Chernobyl computer virus. "Very embarrassing," Tweety Fish admits.

Although ISS had been more than happy to play up the fact that it could detect the software, Dildog fully expected companies would not only reverse-engineer it, they would soon come up with a removal tool. That was why he'd released his software as "open source," which meant hackers the world over could tweak the code to suit their needs. From previous experience, Dildog figured BO2K would then spread like a virus, morphing into perhaps dozens of different versions. He counted more than 300,000 downloads of the original Back Orifice, which ran solely on Windows 95 and 98 and was spread primarily by e-mail attachment. Who knew how many other copies had been spread friend to friend, hacker to hacker, "cracker" to victim? Dildog didn't care. Like Louis Malle, the French film director who once said, "I like confusion, but it drives the crew crazy," Dildog enjoyed anarchy and confusion, believing the question was usually more important than the answer.

In a hacker's eyes, only one thing could be worse than dealing with a corporation, and that would be breakfasting with law enforcement. A number of geeks complain that FBI agents have stormed into their homes, waving warrants and confiscating computers. "And the feds never seem to get around to returning your stuff either," says Maiffret, who was raided by the feds in 1998. "Even if they did give it back, the way technology changes it would just be old tech anyway. So it's really a way of them to punish you without actually having to go to the trouble of taking you to court." Just dealing with an allegation can cost $2,000 to $5,000, and perhaps $20,000 to deal with more serious legal issues. Or more.

Kevin Mitnick's defense team, which was paid a fraction of what it usually earns to defend the star-crossed computer addict, billed the government for 3,000 hours of work over three years but put in more than double that. At the usual L.A. lawyer rates, that would have meant Mitnick's bill, if he'd paid legal retail, would have topped $2 million. Why did his case drag on so long? Because "prosecutors [were] trying to make an example of him," surmises Jennifer Granick, a San Francisco lawyer who has defended a number of hackers.

What had Mitnick done to land him five years in jail? The indictment alleged he had copied proprietary computer and cellphone software code from Motorola, Nokia, and Sun, worth, the government claimed, $80 million. In essence, prosecutors were charging him with economic espionage before there was a law against it. Mitnick, who was sentenced to a halfway house as a teenager for treatment for an obsession with computers, admits he hoarded this information but never shared it with anyone. He claims he wanted to study it.

"When he was in jail his eyes would shine whenever we would talk about computer code," says Brian Martin, aka "Jericho," webmaster of attrition.org, a site that tracks computer crime, and a former member of the Mitnick defense's computer forensics team. How did Mitnick, known less for his computer skills and more for his verbal dexterity, score his software fix? With Motorola, he says, it was easy. One day on his way home after work he stopped at a pay phone and, posing as an engineer, demanded the source code to a new cell phone. "A few minutes later I called back and was told it was already being transmitted to an online account I'd given them," Mitnick says. By the time he got home he had scored the blueprints to Motorola's latest product.

For a pretty abstract kind of crime, the government's tactics were heavy-handed, as if it were dealing with a terrorist. Mitnick wasn't just denied bail, he was denied a bail hearing. Donald Randolph, Mitnick's court-appointed attorney, says he had never heard of that before in his twenty-five years of practice. It took almost a year, and a number of motions filed by Randolph, before the prosecution turned over the nine gigabytes of electronic evidence it had accumulated, so the defense could prepare its case. Prosecutors were reluctant to give Mitnick a laptop to prepare his defense. Much of the rationale for the delay was the unfounded fear that somehow Mitnick could—without a modem—wreak cyberhavoc from prison. Indeed, prison officials had imbued Mitnick with powers befitting James Bond. He was once stowed in solitary confinement because prison officials were afraid he could turn his Walkman into an FM transmitter that could be used to bug the warden's office.

When legal historians look back on Mitnick's case, they may be left scratching their heads over some of Judge Mariana Pfaelzer's odder rulings. It is with the issue of encryption that the Mitnick case really broke new ground. "This may be the first case in which encryption issues were litigated in a criminal arena," says Randolph of the Santa Monica, California–based firm Randolph & Levanas. "But get ready, it's going to be a regular issue starting now." Especially after the Department of Justice had for a time tossed around a very bad idea called the "Cyberspace Electronic Security Act." The bill was scary for a number of reasons. It would have permitted investigators to secretly enter your home, your private property, and search through your computer, or even install software without your knowledge that could intercept your keystrokes—your passwords, private e-mail conversations, and online chats—or override encryption programs. Fortunately, after word of the proposal leaked out and met a storm of resistance, the Department of Justice quietly buried it.

But it continued to be concerned that criminals would rely more and more on encryption. Unfortunately, its proposed solution would have been like using satellite surveillance to nab a purse-snatcher. Of course, the irony was not lost on hackers: The Department of Justice was asking permission to breach Americans' computer systems while at the same time it went after people who breached Americans' computer systems, American companies, and the American government.

With Mitnick, the issue centered around a section of encrypted data found on the laptop in his possession when he was arrested in 1995. Since the prosecution couldn't crack the code, they said they wouldn't turn it over to the defense as discovery until Mitnick handed over the encryption key. The judge agreed. "In essence, the prosecution was arguing that their ignorance provides the justification for withholding evidence," Randolph says. "To the best of our knowledge, never before had this tactic been attempted." The reason Mitnick's attorneys wanted to see the evidence, besides their constitutional right to do so, was to see if there was any evidence that would point to Mitnick's innocence. If, for instance, he got the Motorola cell phone source code from a source other than Motorola, he would not be guilty of computer fraud. (He might have been in receipt of stolen property, but that would have been a misdemeanor.) And Motorola's source code, and Sun's and Nokia's, had been floating around hacker circles for years.

What was the result of the well-publicized treatment Kevin Mitnick received? Hundreds of attacks on corporate, government, and military web sites protesting his treatment, with web sites like kevinmitnick.com and freekevin.com spreading the latest Kevin Mitnick news. Much of the reporting, naturally, derided law enforcement.

Martin even posted this joke on attrition.org: The NSA, the CIA, and the FBI all want to prove they are the best at apprehending criminals, so the president gives them a test. He releases a rabbit into the forest and commands each of them to catch it. The NSA places animal informants throughout the forest and interrogates all plant and mineral witnesses. After three months of extensive investigations, it concludes that rabbits do not exist. The CIA, after two weeks with no leads, burns down the forest, killing everything in it, including the rabbit, which an unnamed agency source announces had it coming. The FBI takes only two hours to emerge from the forest with a badly beaten bear. The bear is yelling: "Okay, okay, I'm a rabbit, I'm a rabbit."

Hackers are always on red alert for the FBI. In fact, when Maiffret was contacted over the Internet by the alleged terrorist Khalid Ibrahim, a member of Harkat-ul-Ansar, a militant Indian separatist group on the State Department's list of the thirty most dangerous terrorist organizations in the world, he assumed Ibrahim worked for the feds. There are myriad reasons law enforcement has not been up to the task of combating digital crime. First, there is the dot com brain drain. The best and brightest take their pensions and jump to tech companies that pay three times their annual government salary. (You never hear of a top chief technology officer leaving his six-figure job to take a position with the FBI.) Or they start their own consultant firms. Law enforcement agents are also hampered by the realities of cyberspace. Unlike a crime scene in the real world, you can't seal off the entire computer network to a massive e-commerce site like Yahoo! Traditional crime-solving methods that have proved successful against terrorism and street crime don't work in the vagaries of cyberspace. Yet the FBI is stretched so thin, it often sends street agents to cover computer crime cases, the type of people who wouldn't know a URL from a UFO. Which is why the Bureau is viewed in such a dim light on-line. "The FBI is clueless when it comes to hackers," says Martin. "Their idea of a crime strategy is to track down rumors over the Internet in the hopes that someone is dumb enough to admit something."

This was the method FBI agents used to track the person they thought had committed the February 2000 denial of service attacks. A week after the first wave, the FBI thought it had found its malicious geek: a pimply-faced twenty-year-old script kiddie with low-level computer skills who, investigators believed, launched the electronic barrage from his job in tech support at a major auto parts supplier in Dearborn, Michigan. Although speculation had been running wild as to the identity of the culprit, hackers, crackers, pirates, and thieves treading on the seamy side of cyberspace were committing "serial bragging": taking credit for the attacks on hacker chat channels. Many had blithely assumed the name "MafiaBoy," one of the potential perps mentioned in a stream of news stories about the investigation. There were dozens of MafiaBoys running around the Internet in the days and weeks after the DOS. But one hacker wannabe stood out from the rest. "Pig Farmer," also known as "Eurostylin" and "Bean Farmer," had e-mailed Martin at the attrition site (he said he was a fan) right after the first wave of attacks, bragging about his exploits. When he couldn't answer simple questions about the assaults, however, he was dismissed as yet another crackpot craving the limelight.

As the real culprits unleashed torrents of electronic packets at more e-commerce sites over the course of the week—Amazon, Charles Schwab, Datek, ZDNet, and Lycos, among many others—Pig Farmer widened his contacts, sending mail from America Online to dozens of journalists in the hopes someone would listen to him. But nobody would. In an Internet Relay Chat (IRC) with some alleged cronies, Pig Farmer, ostensibly named because his parents have a farm where they raise pigs, beans, and corn, wrote: "I have sent 15 journalists an e-mail so we can get our message out. They have not responded to us, but the ones who have say we are not legit but we'll show them." He also brashly claimed he would hit CNN and Time Warner the next day, and they were attacked.

When Martin asked him after the first wave of attacks why he was doing this, Pig Farmer responded: "If you notice the targets, They are all PUBLICLY traded companies, This was an attempt to put a 'Scare' into internet stock holders." But without hard evidence, Martin still couldn't be sure. He then passed on the e-mail that Pig Farmer had sent him to James M. Atkinson, founder of Granite Island Group of Gloucester, Massachusetts, a company that specializes in technical surveillance countermeasures. Atkinson, in addition to conducting bug sweeps of corporations, is also an expert hacker tracker. Because Atkinson has close ties to law enforcement, he knew agents that had nothing on Pig Farmer and that the FBI was floundering in its investigation of the DOS attacker. All he had to start with was Pig Farmer's e-mail, which was a shame. It was no way to conduct an investigation. But Atkinson decided he would donate a few days of his time to see if he could help out.

It took almost no time for him to locate Pig Farmer's file directories and home page on AOL, complete with pictures of a barn, trailer, and souped-up car. Atkinson, who conducted hundreds of analysis projects like this, was not in the business of catching digital criminals. His company focused on bug sweeps, wiretap detection, and the protection of corporations and government agencies from illegal surveillance or technical espionage.

"It took me 23 minutes to find out who the guy was," Atkinson says. "The way you catch mischief makers is you look for minutiae and small mistakes they make. When Pig Farmer reached out to media people, he left a trail that led back to him."

On the AOL home page, Atkinson found a photo of a bright red 1999 Dodge sports car with chrome wheels and, most important, tinted windows. Pig Farmer had deleted the license number from the photo, but he kept the car waxed and shiny and Atkinson was able to extract an image of his target by taking a photo of his car with a Sony digital camera using a flash in bright sunlight. Pig Farmer had received a ticket for the tinted windows, something he seemed proud of since he tried to unsuccessfully scan the image into his home page. But the file got corrupted. Of a 680-kilobyte file, only 630K got through. Atkinson downloaded the entire site into his Silicon Graphics workstation and recovered the fragments of the damaged document. On the ticket, he had eradicated his name and address, but not the number on the ticket, nor the license number of his car, the date, or the time. Atkinson made a call to the Michigan State Police and within nineteen minutes an officer phoned back with the potential perp's name, address, and other relevant information.

Pig Farmer "bragged about the attacks before, during and after," Atkinson says. "He seemed to do everything he could to draw attention to himself." With Janet Reno screaming behind the scenes that she wanted to hold a press conference announcing an arrest, the FBI got more than a dozen subpoenas and brought Pig Farmer in for questioning. But it didn't take long for agents and Department of Justice attorneys to realize all they had was a twenty-year-old hacker wannabe who had wasted their time. Pig Farmer had been reading everything he could of the DOS attacks through the media, then immediately crowed about it online in chat channels and through e-mails. If bragging were a crime, Pig Farmer might be serving a life sentence. Instead, the feds had to let him go.

Of course, "if hackers didn't brag, I wouldn't have a job," says a man who goes by the initials "J3." J3 trolls the hacker underground, monitoring discussion channels on Internet Relay Chat, checking out the latest info on "phreaking"—cracking the phone system—dialing up bulletin boards, and checking out web sites that offer password-cracking software and how-to guides. For J3 this isn't just a hobby, it's a job. The computer security firm ICSA hired him to act as a kind of hacker spy. When he gets wind of a new security hole, he passes the information on to ICSA's tech staff so that the company can either develop a defense or tip off software makers before the flaw can be exploited. "I've found a company's entire password file posted to a web site, or that hackers have root in a network or that a merchant site with a database of credit cards has been compromised," he says. "I then contact the companies and warn them."

Yet the hacks keep on coming, and law enforcement has had little success in catching those responsible. That indicates that despite the contentious relationship between hackers and corporate America it's only a matter of time before spies turn to the Internet to siphon away valuable R&D from business competitors. It doesn't take William Gibson–like imagination to see why cyberspace will be the corporate battleground of the future.

The rise of colossal databases and innovations in data-sifting technologies have created an informational glut, with the spread of the web the final step. A talented hacker can uncover corporate secrets instantly with a few taps of the keyboard. For decades this information rested in remote mainframes difficult to access, even for the ones who put it there, or were filed away in dusty cabinets at corporate headquarters. The move to desktop PCs and local servers in the 1990s has distributed this data far and wide. Computers now hold half a billion bank accounts, half a billion credit card accounts, 200 million credit history files (approximately one for each American over eighteen), hundreds of millions of mortgage and retirement funds, medical claims, and more. That's just on the consumer end. There are also thousands of corporate computer networks accessible from the outside over phone lines, since employees have to be able to dial in remotely. But letting in some and keeping out others, while providing basics like e-mail and Internet surfing, is challenging. No amount of computer security has been able to keep hackers out. If a company has a web site, it is vulnerable to a computer miscreant sneaking in right through the company's virtual welcome mat: its home page.

This was how a lone fifteen-year-old tenth-grader from suburban America cracked India's most important nuclear research center in Bombay in May 1998. He was watching TV coverage of India's underground nuclear tests and for some reason it stuck in his craw. He was not sure exactly why. After all, he was much too young to remember Hiroshima, Nagasaki, and the Cuban missile crisis. He couldn't even find India on the map. Some Third World hole that couldn't even feed its own people was getting into a nuclear arms race with Pakistan and China. The more he thought about it, the madder he got, so he decided to wreak vengeance on the Indians. And he would accomplish this without leaving his bedroom. In cyberspace, where the young hacker spent much of his life, he went by the nickname "t3k-9," pronounced "Tech-9." He was especially adept at cracking passwords and log-ins, the keys to illegally accessing computer systems. On this particular day, t3k-9 stomped upstairs carrying his favorite hack snacks—chocolate Pop Tarts, Coca-Cola, and sour jawbreakers—and went to his bedroom, where he booted up his computer and listened to the comforting squawk of his modem. He checked in with search engine Infoseek and plugged in ".in atomic," the equivalent of typing "India, atomic research." One of the first sites to come up was India's Bhabha Atomic Research Center (BARC), which he had read had been instrumental in helping India develop the A-bomb.

He pointed and clicked his way to the BARC site and accessed the John the Ripper DES Encryption Cracker software he had downloaded off the Internet, where literally thousands of complex hacker applications and "how-to" guides are available from web sites and hacker chat channels. The password cruncher worked by setting up a phony log-in program so that BARC thought it was accepting a connection from a friendly machine. Then, by brute force, the cruncher tried every single combination of letters and numbers until it hit the jackpot.

First, the application ran through all the lettered combinations at the speed of digital light—a, b, aa, bb, cc—then, after going through the entire alphabet, backtracking to ab, ac, ad, and so forth. t3k-9 had also added special customized word lists that combined letters and numbers he'd downloaded over the course of his travels. Forty-five seconds after he'd started, t3k-9 was amazed to discover that he'd cracked one of the passwords. He was inside India's number one atomic research network. His eyes bugged. He checked the password: "ANSI." Someone's name, he thought, the same as the log-in prompt. He couldn't believe his luck. The administrator hadn't followed standard password selection rules, which would have meant complex strings of numbers and letters—more difficult to crack because the longer it takes, the greater the likelihood you'll get caught.

t3k-9's first step was to download all the passwords and log-in names. Then he installed a back door that would enable him to gain entry into the system without being detected. After that, he consulted the network map, which was open to public display. He headed over to the web server and read through e-mails written in scientific geek-speak, then riffled through some documents on particle physics. Boring stuff, he thought. He decided to get out while the getting was good, downloading a few e-mails and a scientific document for souvenirs. Then, after erasing logs to ensure no one would be able to track him, he logged off.

If he'd kept this to himself, no one would have ever known. And in the days to follow, India's top nuclear research facility would probably never have suffered the ignominy of perhaps 100 hackers running roughshod through its computer network like gangs on a rampage. But t3k-9 couldn't keep mum. He did what every self-respecting hacker would do. He bragged. He posted the whole BARC password file—all 800 passwords and log-in names—on one of the hacker channels. Immediately, hackers began accessing this information and attacked Bhabha. Within days hackers from all over the world were wilding through the research center's computer systems, deleting files and copying e-mails, including one that questioned the legitimacy of one of the explosions, and tearing down the web site, replacing it with a mushroom cloud and a giggly greeting. If t3k-9 had been a terrorist or corporate spy instead of a kid who found physics papers lame, who knows what he could have downloaded.

Thus far, corporations have shown much less imagination than t3k-9, although they are beginning to keep tabs on their rivals over the Net: "We know our competitors check out our web site because we track their domain names," says Michael Renda, a manager of Internet projects at AlliedSignal. "And of course, we do the same to them." The Net makes it a snap to check out a competitor—its prices, customer lists, suppliers, distributors, and new product information, because companies are caught between two conflicting missions: providing customer and partner information available over the Internet and at the same time protecting their proprietary information.

DuPont, on its web site, offers anyone with access to a computer and a modem a list of every factory and yarn spinner the company uses in the production of the fabric CoolMax, which is used in athletic apparel. "They list factories and yarn spinners, their addresses, plant managers," says Mary Ellen Bates of Bates Information Services of Washington, D.C. "You can call suppliers—are they paying you enough, asking you to provide a new fabric, threatening to move operations to Shanghai? If you want to make a competing product you try to schmooze the plant managers. I don't see why it's beneficial to DuPont to display this kind of stuff."

Rumors abound on the Net about hackers being hired by corporations to steal proprietary information or money, but cases that come to public light are rare. Companies have been known to get victimized over the Internet in other ways, however. Until recently corporations parked whole divisions of employees and their direct report chain on their web sites, along with corporate profiles and résumés. Boeing, on its web site, listed the personnel of whole divisions, hundreds and hundreds of workers, including those who worked on technology used in the space shuttle. The aerospace company's web site used to be "a gold mine for a competitor that would like to hire away staff who come with lots of sensitive information," says Robert D. Aaron of the Atlanta-based research firm Aaron/Smith Associates. "And you know who to talk to about each person. You can call up their boss, work your way up the organizational chart, and find out information about an executive, his background, how he is to work for." Eventually Boeing got wise and pulled this material.

To a hacker like Chameleon, however, accessing harder-to-get information requires more talent and skill. Before Maiffret escaped a severe addiction to hacking to grab a lucrative chunk of the dot com craze, he spent most of his days locked in his room in the southern California suburban home he shared with his mother and sister, plugged into his computer for thirty-six-hour-long hack sprees, probing networks to learn about the latest architectures, Internet servers, software exploit scripts and techniques, coding and decoding software, chatting up girls via e-mail and instant messaging, including one virtual relationship that he says ended disastrously, and dissecting back issues of *Phrack,* an online hacker zine.

Only when he couldn't keep his eyelids propped open any longer would he pull himself away from his virtual existence, crawl across the carpet to a corner of his room, and curl up on a comforter to catch some REM. "I preferred sleeping on the floor because I rarely slept," Maiffret recalls. School wasn't relevant. He stopped attending. The twenty-four-hour clock lost meaning; his life had been shaped into two seamless parts: cyberspace and sleep.

Not only was Chameleon known for his technical skills and respected as an "elite," or in the digital lexicon of the Net, "3l33t" hacker, he also viewed himself as a kind of twenty-first-century electronic poet and political activist. When he cracked a U.S. Department of Defense web site dedicated to artificial intelligence, he wrote: "It's funny how people go through life searching for the truth, yet when they find it they wish they hadn't searched for it. The truth is a virus and people don't want to get it. Live and deal with the truth, because sooner or later you will have to face it." For fun, Chameleon slipped in a piece of software that played the whistly theme to the *X-Files* every time someone accessed the page.

His first brush with fame came when he was seventeen, and ironically, for something he didn't do. At the time, Chameleon was affiliated with a hacker band called Noid, with whom he had penetrated dozens of corporate networks, joyriding around the computers, riffling through servers and files, "to see how things worked," Maiffret says. At the time, the big news in computer security was that a hacker group called the Masters of Downloading (MOD) had stolen a piece of military software called DEM, or the Defense Information Systems Network Equipment Manager.

CBS News managed to get word to MOD, but since members were based in Europe, they told CBS to talk to Chameleon. Since he didn't want to do the show alone, Chameleon grabbed his roommate, a "phone phreaker"—someone who manipulates the telephone system to get what he wants—and they marched down to the studio. To protect their identities their faces were shadowed and voices modulated. But Chameleon had no intention of saying anything remotely incriminating, at least nothing true, so he lied. "I never claimed I stole the software; I said MOD did it, because that was true. But I did say I was a member of MOD. Man, and man, what a stupid lie!"

Shortly afterward Chameleon was pinged online. Someone by the name of Ibrahim told him he wanted the software. He kept messaging Chameleon, saying he'd pay good money for it. "At first I thought it was a guy messing with me; happens all the time on IRC," Chameleon says. "I played along, even though I thought it was b.s. But then the guy told me to check a P.O. box" three towns over from where Chameleon lived in Irvine, California.

When he got there, he peered inside the box. The lone piece of mail was a pink slip. A certified letter. This meant he had to sign for it. Which meant if the guy was an undercover agent, Chameleon could be in big trouble. He and his Noid boys had been extra busy lately, having defaced a slew of web sites in recent weeks. "We had gone on a spree, ten or twelve sites, including the Army, Navy, Air Force—hell, we hacked one of each of the three branches of the military," Chameleon says. But he also realized his interactions with Ibrahim had been 100 percent legal, at least from his side. "Even if he was FBI, I hadn't given him software or anything," Chameleon says. So he opened up the box, grabbed the pink slip, marched up to the counter and accepted two $500 money orders. Written on the envelope was a pager number, a contact in Chicago. Chameleon wadded up the envelope and chucked it in the trash.

Okay, maybe the guy is a terrorist, Chameleon thought, or maybe he's FBI. Nevertheless, he filled out the money orders and cashed them at a bank down the street. "I would never rip anyone off but I had no problem doing it to a terrorist. Besides, that was a hell of a lot of money for me back then," he says. He took most of his booty and bought a Nintendo 64 game for his mentally handicapped sister, since "the doctors told me any toy that requires hand-eye coordination would be good for her." He used the rest to tool around town and fly up to San Jose to visit a friend. Meanwhile Ibrahim kept trying to raise him over IRC, the messages becoming more threatening. "I gave you money and what the fuck? I don't want to have to go back to my people and tell them you ripped us off," Ibrahim wrote.

Afraid, Chameleon stopped venturing online.

But this didn't prevent him from waking up with a jolt a few mornings after, a gun nuzzling his temple.

Afterword

We are happy to report it wasn't Ibrahim and a gang of henchmen who stormed Maiffret's home and terrorized his sister, confronted his mother in the shower, and woke him up at gunpoint.

It was the FBI.

Agents confiscated Maiffret's computer equipment, worth about $3,000. "They never gave it back and I was never charged with any crime," Maiffret says. He believes they had been watching him for months, "sniffing his network connection," but isn't sure whether it was his activities with Noid or Ibrahim that attracted their attention. A few weeks after the raid, Maiffret borrowed a laptop from a friend. Ibrahim had been trying to contact him. Meanwhile, the Pentagon hit a suspected terrorist training camp in Afghanistan run by Islamic militant Osama bin Laden with cruise missiles. When nine members of Harkat-ul-Ansar were killed, Ibrahim's group declared war on the United States. For months after, Ibrahim tried to reestablish contact. But Maiffret made it a point never to talk to him again.

Maiffret, like many American teenagers, just wouldn't take Ibrahim seriously. He mocks authority. He is headstrong. He draws his own conclusions. He doesn't like to be told what to do. The same attributes that make him a top-notch hacker also render him a high-risk corporate operative, says Maiffret, whose boutique Internet security firm, eEye, is thriving.

The first hacker to pierce India's nuke researcher center, t3k-9, told me he can't wait for the day a corporation will pay him $100,000 to hack. But could he be trusted not to boast of his exploits?

Karim Fadel, the trade show spy who felt guilty about what he did, quit PictureTel and, like Maiffret, has taken full advantage of the dot com boom. He accepted a CI position with a company tucked inside Washington, D.C.'s tech beltway and says he doesn't rule out applying tactics he learned at PictureTel.

Jan Herring, the former CIA star who founded the first business intelligence spy unit at Motorola, continues to consult and teach open-source collection techniques. He is a regular speaker at conferences sponsored by SCIP, the organization he formed to preach his business intelligence gospel.

Liz Lightfoot quit Teltech to take a job as the director of research for Gartner Institute, a Minneapolis startup that builds certification programs to improve the credentials of corporate tech staff.

Ed O'Malley, the former FBI agent who warned the French DGSE about the Economic Espionage Act, runs his own CI consultancy.

What befell former CIA swashbuckler Dewey Clarridge? He transferred his skills to the private sector after resigning from the agency. He is now an arms dealer. His specialty: missiles.

Avery Dennison was furious with Victor Lee for violating his agreement. He had promised not to testify in any way against the company, but when Lee, on the stand, admitted he had removed confidential markings from documents he mailed to Taiwan, he undermined the government's case. His fate was sealed during the discovery phase of the civil trial Avery was pursuing against Four Pillars. That's when lawyers learned that Lee had neglected to turn over to Agent Bartholomew the final two pages of a six-page letter to Yang, and had redacted another: "Buying books is easy," he had written, but "getting secret or confidential documents is harder." His punishment: six months at a halfway house and home confinement, which, to add to the ignominy, he would pay for himself (the ankle bracelet ran $4.35 a day). Worse, Avery named him as a codefendant in the $40 million judgment it won against Four Pillars, the one thing (besides jail) he had tried to avoid all along. "I hope Lee is sweating," says Zwillinger. "He deserves it."

After the verdict Sally Yang winged it back to Taiwan to be with her husband; P. Y. returned to his Cleveland apartment to serve out the rest of his sentence alone. All told, he spent two years under house arrest in America while Avery decapitated his company in China. The civil verdict was a slam dunk after the guilty vote in the criminal trial, resulting in a $40 million judgment against the Yangs, Lee, and Four Pillars Enterprises. Meanwhile, both cases are under appeal. Some legal experts believe there is a good chance the criminal verdict will be overturned.

Marc Zwillinger left the Department of Justice to move to the private sector. He is now with Kirkland and Ellis, heading its cyber-crime section.

Nancy Luque and Eric Dubelier continue to press forward on the appeals process for the Yangs. They also take on an astonishing number of white-collar cases.

Marc Barry is involved in a joint venture with Raytheon, building a $7 million war room and running intelligence capers for his company, C³I Analytics in New York. He would like to dedicate this book to his Aunt Shirley and Uncle Brian Barry, who throughout his childhood tried to teach him that no one likes a sneak . . . in hindsight, he says, "Thank God I never listened to you people."

Adam Penenberg would like to dedicate this book with love to his father, who passed away during the writing of it, and to his mother, who is no doubt at this very moment updating her web site.

Adam L. Penenberg and Marc Barry
New York City
May 2000

Index

Aaron, Robert D., 172
ACS. *See* Advanced Competitive
    Strategies
Advanced Competitive Strategies
    (ACS), 20–21
Aethra Telecomunicazioni, 87
Akron Beacon Journal, 130
Alcoa, 42
Allende, 31
Allen, Thomas, 47–48, 61, 62, 66
AlliedSignal, 109, 120, 124, 171
Alta Vista, 116
Amazon.com, 132, 154, 166
American Express, 43
American Voice Mail, 77
Ampex, 38
Analyzer. *See* Tenebaum, Ehud
Ancker, Fred, 119, 122
Andrews, Gerald, 16
Anheuser-Busch, 124–125
"Answering machine pick," 19
Apple computers, 10, 43
Aquarius project, 60
Army (U.S.), 20
AroSurgical, 155
Asia, 49, 75
    and Avery Dennison market, 47–48,
      102, 106, 150
    See also China; Japan; Taiwan
Association of Consulting Chemists
    and Chemical Engineers, 122
Atkinson, James M., 166–167

attrition.org, 162, 164, 165
Automobile industry, 27, 114, 121,
    122–123
Avery Dennison, xi–xv, 178–179
    Asian market, 47–48, 102, 106, 150
    confidentiality agreements, 57–58
    and FBI, xii–xiii, 62–63, 69–70, 133
    history, 50–52
    trial of Yangs, 128, 133–134, 135
    See also Four Pillars Enterprises; Lee,
      Ten Hong (Victor)
Avery, R. Stanton, xiv, 51

Back Orifice, 158–161
BackWeb, 87
Ballistic Missile Defense Advanced
    Technology Center, 10
BARC. *See* Bhabha Atomic Research
    Center
Barry, Marc, 75–84, 94, 179
Barry, Marion, 104
Bartholomew, Michael, xiii, 63–64,
    145, 147, 149, 178
BASF, 109, 120
Bates, Mary Ellen, 172
Bausch & Lomb, 75
Bayer, 120, 124
Bean Farmer. *See* Pig Farmer
Beer industry. *See* Beverage industry
Bell, William, 10
Bellcore, 94
Berlin Wall, 14–15

181